SUPPORTING LITERACIES FOR CHILDREN OF COLOR

A comprehensive theory-to-practice guidebook, *Supporting Literacies for Children of Color* argues for a new strength-based view of teaching to support the literacy talents and abilities of preschool-aged children of Color.

The early childhood field is at a critical juncture in preschool literacy education as educators confront an ever-changing array of curricular approaches and assessment measures while still trying to meet the social, cultural, language, and literacy needs of individual children. By integrating parent and teacher literacy perspectives, as well as calling on the author's own decades of teaching, this book offers practical tools and strategies for culturally responsive pedagogy and demonstrates effective methods for using oral language and multilingualism to celebrate and deepen the literacy capabilities of children of Color.

Featuring examples of children's literacy processes and products both at home and in preschools to illustrate effective instructional strategies, as well as boxes noting important ideas and strategies in each major section, this text will guide students and educators toward creating a supportive learning environment for children of Color.

Daniel R. Meier is Professor of Elementary Education at San Francisco State University, USA, and works as a literacy instructor in local preschools. He is the co-author of *Documentation and Inquiry in the Early Childhood Classroom* (Routledge, 2017) and co-editor of *Narrative Inquiry in Early Childhood and Elementary School* (Routledge, 2016), *Educational Change in International Early Childhood Contexts* (Routledge, 2014), and *Nature Education With Young Children* (Routledge, 2013).

SUPPORTING LITERACIES FOR CHILDREN OF COLOR

A Strength-Based Approach to Preschool Literacy

Daniel R. Meier

Routledge
Taylor & Francis Group

NEW YORK AND LONDON

First published 2020
by Routledge
52 Vanderbilt Avenue, New York, NY 10017

and by Routledge
2 Park Square, Milton Park, Abingdon, Oxon, OX14 4RN

Routledge is an imprint of the Taylor & Francis Group, an informa business

© 2020 Taylor & Francis

Library of Congress Cataloging-in-Publication Data
A catalog record for this book has been requested

ISBN: 978-0-367-11185-4 (hbk)
ISBN: 978-0-367-11186-1 (pbk)
ISBN: 978-0-429-02519-8 (ebk)

Typeset in Bembo
by Apex CoVantage, LLC

In memory of my grandparents, who knew languages and literacies though not formal schooling

CONTENTS

AUTHOR BIOGRAPHY

Daniel R. Meier is Professor of Elementary Education at San Francisco State University. He teaches in the M.A. program in early childhood education, the Multiple Subject Teaching Credential Program, and the Ed.D. program in educational leadership. Meier teaches courses in reading/language arts, multilingual development, narrative inquiry and memoir, qualitative research, and international education. Meier received his B.A. in English literature from Wesleyan University, Ed.M. in reading and language from Harvard University, and Ph.D. in language and literacy from the Graduate School of Education, University of California at Berkeley. He is the author of numerous articles and several books on early childhood education, language and literacy, international education, and reflective practice and teacher research. Meier is the co-author, most recently, of *Documentation and Inquiry in the Early Childhood Classroom: Research Stories of Engaged Practitioners in Urban Centers and Schools* (2017, Routledge) and *Narrative Inquiry in Early Childhood and Elementary School: Learning to Teach, Teaching Well* (2016, Routledge). He works as a part-time literacy instructor in the Berkeley Unified School District, and co-facilitates the Las Americas Early Education School Inquiry Group, San Francisco Unified School District. Meier is also at work on a project examining learning stories as authentic assessment in California, and the role of digital stories in literacy learning in preschools in the San Francisco Bay area and the West Bank/Palestine.

ACKNOWLEDGMENTS

I would like to thank all of the children, teachers, and families who contributed to this book. Without their support and participation, there would be no book. I specifically thank these teachers and families – Prenties Brown, Maria Carriedo, Carlos Castillejo, Jamal Cooks, Shyla Crowder, Dawn Douangsawang, Isauro Michael Escamilla, Sahara Gonzalez-Garcia, Amanda Ibarra, Mr. Jon Sims, Gaya Kekulawela, Ambreen Khawaja, Dale Long, Alma Lyons, Hannah Nguyen, Haneefah Shuaibe-Peters, and Maria Sujo. They graciously gave of their time to speak with me about their views on the literacy talents and abilities of preschool children of Color, and gave me permission to use their literacy teaching as examples in this book. I also thank the following individuals who read and commented on some of the early chapters of this book – Lauren Arend, Laura Dariola, and Maria del Rosario Zavala. Thanks also to Michelle Chinn for her help with editing and fact-checking, and a huge thank you to the editorial and production team at Routledge. I am truly lucky to publish with this great group. Thanks, too, to Gerald Campano for taking the time out of his summer to write the Foreword. Last, I thank my family – Hazelle, Kaili, and Toby – for their support and encouragement.

FOREWORD

In the elementary school where I taught for a number of years in California's Central Valley, with students of predominantly Mexican, Filipino, Hmong, Cambodian, and African descent, there was a district "gifted and talented" program for which less than 1% of the children "qualified." When I moved to the Midwest for my first university faculty position, the school near my house, serving predominately white families, also had a gifted and talented program, and there 80% of the children were "qualified." It even had a "profoundly gifted and talented program" serving an additional 10% of the students.

Putting aside for the moment critiques of whether "gifted and talented programs" should even exist, there are no ethics or reasoning that can justify this difference in educational access and equity, which mirrors larger racialized social stratifications. There was abundant evidence, of course, to suggest all the children in both schools were brilliant. The children in the Midwestern school excelled on many levels, including standard academic measures, inquiry projects, and the arts. In the California school, in addition to having high standardized test scores, many of the children in my class were developing multiple languaging practices, and using literacy as a vehicle to engage in profound social critique, including critiques of the educational system itself, drawing from the intellectual, cultural, and activist legacies of their communities. Nevertheless, in one school, it was normal for the school to position the children as "struggling" and having a deficit. In the other, it was normal to be "gifted."

In *Supporting Literacies for Children of Color: A Strength-Based Approach to Preschool Literacy Education*, Daniel R. Meier, a veteran educator and critical researcher who has been working in the field of early childhood literacy for decades, is making an intervention into these types of injustices at the level of teaching and learning in classrooms. The book offers an important and much needed resource for early childhood educators, and is both practical and theoretically informed. Meier canvasses longstanding ideas in early childhood literacy and puts them in conversation with frameworks on culturally relevant and sustaining pedagogies, critical race theory, and emergent multilingualism, to name a few. He also offers very practical illustrations of powerful teaching and learning in prose that is both lucid and engaging. Importantly, Meier highlights what he has learned from many of the parents and educators with whom he had been collaborating, further breaking down the dichotomies between theory and practice, home and school, and research and teaching.

Not unlike many educators, I myself became particularly interested in early childhood literacy as a field when I became a parent. This is a role that arrived a little later in life than I had anticipated. After decades of teaching and researching literacy from a critical-sociocultural perspective, I gained a renewed appreciation of the sophisticated forms of sense-making and world-making young children engage in as part of their everyday lives. And their full lives – both in and outside of school – are ineluctably shaped by larger societal forces and dynamics, including race, gender, (dis)ability, generation, language, immigration, and histories of colonization and enslavement, which in turn are mediated by early childhood educators, at once one of the most important and undervalued of professions. My own four-year-old child, Gabriela, was born during a period of resurgent right-wing populism and white supremacy in the United States and around the world. Gabriela is a child of Argentinian, German, and Filipino descent whose extended care network reflects the world of multiplicity and difference to which this populism is a reaction. Her best friend and first cousin from Queens, New York, is Afro-Latinx, with roots in South America, the Bronx, and the Caribbean. Gabriela has other young relatives who have multiple roots from Italy, Lebanon, Germany, North Africa, and Mindanao, just to name a few of what the philosopher Édouard Glissant (2010) might have characterized as the rhizomatic identities of so many of the children in places such as New York City, Philadelphia, the Bay Area (where Daniel Meier works), and increasingly suburban and rural areas around the country. The lived experiences and literate practices of these young children are a powerful resistance to the separatism, racism, and xenophobia that too often characterize our public discourse, and it is imperative that they be educated in schools which honor their full brilliance.

Gabriela is also participating in an intergenerational, community-based research project which involves families and community members from Indonesian, Latinx, and African-American backgrounds. In investigating educational inequities, they have always expressed the goal of working with educators to bring about educational change. My hope is that they can engage Daniel Meier and his colleagues through a mutual exchange of ideas, as we all find ways for schools to work in solidarity with families of color.

Gerald Campano

Reference

Glissant, E. (2010). *Poetics of relation* (B. Wing, Trans.). Ann Arbor, MI: University of Michigan Press.

INTRODUCTION

OPENING REFLECTIONS

- What are a few important ideas that form the foundation for your vision of an effective literacy education?
- What are a few of the most valuable and effective aspects of how you teach literacy? What are your strengths? What are the sources of these strengths?
- In reflecting on your professional training and teaching, what is your understanding of the literacy talents, interests, and abilities of young children of Color and their families?
- Are there any areas that you want to strengthen in terms of understanding and supporting the literacy education of preschool children of Color?

The Book's Goals and Purpose

Jacqueline Woodson, in her book *brown girl dreaming* (2014), remembers her three-year-old self, when she recreated a moment of wonder and power and joy in her earliest written language exploration. In this remembered moment of literacy discovery *and* achievement, Woodson notes the importance of emotions ("love"), senses ("curves into a hook"), and social-familial connections ("the way my sister taught me to do") that are at the foundation for the literacy learning for young children of Color. It's a view of literacy for young children of Color that comes from a place of strength, comfort, and power. Woodson also shows us, as early childhood educators, that the formation of a strong literacy identity is always simultaneously about the here-and-now and the what will-come-to-pass. This child-initiated and child-controlled acquisition of new knowledge in socially and culturally affirming ways strengthens the desire and the right of children of Color to succeed on their own terms in their own literacy growth. As early childhood teachers and leaders, we need to support the emerging literacy identities as children of Color and to see and teach these children as engaged, spirited, and successful learners.

In this book, I present a strength-based approach for high-quality literacy education during the preschool years for young children of Color. I define strength-based literacy education as an approach, a way of thinking and teaching, that sensitively and thoughtfully supports the literacy talents, interests, dreams, experiences, and perspectives of young children of Color and their families. In one sense, this vision is *child responsive* and developmentally engaging as children learn about literacies through play, discovery, and their own interests. In another sense, the vision is *culturally responsive* and based upon children's social, cultural, familial, and linguistic talents, world views, and traditions.

A strength-based approach also takes into account the literacy memories, beliefs, and goals of children's families and the full range of their home, community, and educational contexts. As early childhood educators, we play pivotal roles in shaping and enacting an engaging literacy curriculum that connects ourselves to children as literacy consumers and creators. This educational vision is also political, as a strength-based literacy education necessitates investing in the social, cultural, and intellectual capital and resources of young children of Color, and ensuring their educational success and achievement as preschool and lifelong learners.

The book also provides a critical, reflective space for early childhood educators to consider our own literacy histories and perspectives on the literacy talents of children of Color, and to make philosophical and pedagogical changes to improve literacy instruction. Creating agentic opportunities for young children's learning is critical, and we can only achieve this goal of deep and lasting literacy change through our own process of professional inquiry, dialogue, and reflection.

Children of Color

Children of Color live and embody a varied range of cultural, racial, social, historical, and linguistic talents, traditions, values, and perspectives. Since the educators and families with whom I spoke for this book all live in the San Francisco Bay area, this book is based upon the social and literacy lives of the children and families who attend local preschools in contexts that I know well. While the majority of the educators' and families' perspectives on strength-based literacy teaching focus on public preschools, I do include voices and experiences of some teachers and families whose children have or do attend private, independent schools. (Please see the Appendix for the list of the educators and families profiled in this book.)

The educators, families, and children whose voices and experiences are featured in this book represent a range of cultural and racial backgrounds and traditions – African-American, Asian American, Latinx, African, Southeast Indian, and children of "mixed" ethnicity. These groups are fluid and varied. For instance, Latinx children range from children born in the U.S. to parents born in Guatemala, Mexico, Nicaragua, and Honduras and who may speak Spanish, Mam, and other indigenous languages. The children in these local preschools, then, as well as the educators and families of Color with whom I spoke about their views on the literacy talents of children of Color, are not a monolithic group or easily categorized by ancestral lineage, cultural traditions, or racial classification.

Intended Audience for the Book

I wrote this book for both novice and veteran early childhood educators taking early childhood or literacy coursework at the A.A., B.A., or M.A. levels, or participating in ongoing professional development and growth in the areas of language, literacy, and teacher reflection. While the primary audience for the book is preschool teachers, the book will also interest preschool directors, administrators, coaches, and mentors. The research, theory, and practice presented in the book are directly relevant to a range of preschool settings – from play-based to more academically focused, from publicly funded to private, and from multilingual to English-medium settings.

If you are currently working as an educator with children and families of Color in a preschool setting, then this book will be directly and immediately relevant. If you are studying and pursuing a career in preschool education, or you are currently working in a preschool but your site does not include children of Color, I hope you still find this book a valuable source of information, inspiration, and effective practice. If you are a preschool teacher, whether head teacher or assistant at any site, please consider how this book can build upon your current knowledge of transformative literacy education for preschool children of Color, and how you and your colleagues can work together in new ways to tinker with your curriculum and strengthen your literacy teaching and work with families. If you are a current or future preschool supervisor or director, coach or mentor, consider how this book can provide a springboard for you and your colleagues to critique your school's current literacy practices, and to strengthen your school's learning environments, materials, instruction, family outreach, and professional dialogue and collaboration. This book can also be used in a teacher inquiry group, critical friends group, community of practice, or professional learning community setting as a text for collaborative dialogue, reflection, and instructional change.

The Book's Origin

In a moment of serendipity, I came across Sabrina Zirkel and Tabora Johnson's (2016) "Mirror, Mirror on the Wall: A Critical Examination of the Conceptualization of the Study of Black Racial Identity in Education," in which the authors examine and critique research on Black racial identity and educational excellence. Although the authors do not focus on preschool literacy education, they challenged me to think about how I perceive the literacy talents and abilities of young children of Color, how other educators and families do, and how the historical trajectory of early literacy research and practice has contributed to negative, deficit-oriented "damage imagery" (p. 302). To provide a counter-narrative to this dominant narrative, an important goal is to "flip the damage narrative" (Tuck, 2009, as cited by Zirkel & Johnson, 2016, p. 307) and begin our individual and collective journeys toward creating new images and narratives of the literacy talents of children of Color.

I was most intrigued with Zirkel and Johnson's focus on "the history of 'damage' imagery" (p. 307), and I wanted to explore how the continued presence of 'damage imagery' in the early literacy field detracts and derails us from an individual and collective recognition and support of the literacy talents and strengths of children of Color. I reflected on how we might reorient ourselves to recognize and maintain a vibrant perspective of children of Color as strong, capable, and determined literacy users and producers in preschools. This book is a product of my reflections, my conversations with talented educators and families of Color, and my direct work with preschool children in classrooms.

The ultimate goal of this reorientation is systemic change to literacy education in individual preschools and constellations of preschools primarily at the local level. We are often called upon to scale up our literacy teaching and to involve as many schools and children as we can. But this goal, while admirable, is often quite difficult to achieve. Further, if we only think of systemic change on a grand scale, we leave out individual and small groups of educators working to conceptualize and implement change in their daily teaching and administration contexts. It is my intention, then, for this book to provide ideas and practices for individuals and small groups of educators to make changes in conceptualizing and implementing curricula to deepen and strengthen the literacy engagement and achievement of young children of Color.

An important initial part of this effort is reframing our image of the literacy talents and abilities of young children of Color and their families. By strengthening our image of children of Color, we strengthen their visibility in classrooms and schools as highly engaged, high-achieving producers and interpreters of multiple languages and literacies in varied social and cultural contexts. And in elevating the image and visibility of the literacy talents of children of Color, we elevate how and why we conceptualize our literacy education and our own self-image as highly capable, agentic educators bent on literacy and educational change.

As Brian Wright (2018) emphasizes, in arguing for a strength-based approach to the education of young Black boys, "the more we know, the less we make up" (p. 67). The more that we as educators understand in a deep and authentic way the capabilities and strengths of Black boys (and all children of Color), then "these boys are not as much 'at risk' as they are '*at promise*'" [italics added for emphasis] (p. 68). I intend this book to support our individual and collective conceptualization and awareness of the literacy talents and abilities of young children of Color, and to actualize the "promise" of their literacy achievement as well as the "promise" of our own literacy teaching and professional growth.

Children of Color – Historical Trends and Images

The formulation of a strength-based literacy education is predicated on positive and informed images of the ability and motivation of children of Color to achieve at high levels of success. In this process, it is helpful to become aware of historical trends and images that portray young children of Color from a deficit lens. Mary Eleanor Rhodes Hoover (2005), based on comments collected from elementary school teachers regarding their thoughts on the reading achievement of African-American children, grouped the teachers' statements into two deficit-based categories – "blame-the-victim beliefs" and "blame-the-system beliefs." Blame-the-victim beliefs state that children can't learn to read because "the parents don't care," "their language is so broken as to be no language at all," "they're culturally deprived." This view emphasizes what Hoover calls the "notion of difference" and that teachers believed that African-American children don't learn to read well because "they're poor. None of the poor can read – in fact, none of the world's poor can read," "they're not motivated and so they forget how to read," "Black students think academics is 'acting White'" (p. 68). What Hoover calls blame-the-system beliefs are exemplified by systemic reasons such as teachers' comments that "the system is unequal – schooling might as well be forgotten until we change the system to meet the needs of all the people," "the textbooks are biased – they're filled with racism, sexism, elitism, and ageism," and "poverty creates such dysfunctional families and traumatic conditions that students cannot learn to read" (p. 69).

When I reviewed a range of research focused on the early literacy learning of young children of Color for this book, I found some language that continues to persist in the literature that resembles Zirkel and Johnson's (2016) damage imagery and Mary Eleanor Rhodes Hoover's findings regarding blame-the-victim beliefs and blame-the-system beliefs.

PERSISTENT DEFICIT TERMS IN SELECTED EARLY LITERACY RESEARCH

Homes and Communities

- "low-income immigrant"
- "disadvantaged"

- "single-parent"
- "low parental educational attainment"
- "lacking enrichment experiences"

Education and Schooling

- "low-achieving"
- "lack of focus"
- "behavioral issues"
- "low-performing"
- "at-risk for school failure"

Language

- "limited English"
- "low-income dual language"
- "limited proficiency"
- "lacking rich conversations"
- "lacking vocabulary"

Literacy

- "lacking book language"
- "lacking knowledge of the written language register"
- "divergent storytellers"
- "unaware of print as a symbol system"
- "lacking access to fiction and nonfiction books"

Taken as a whole, these research trends emphasize what children of Color lack and where they are not in their development versus an authentic picture of their existing talents and their rightful developmental place in literacy acquisition. In light of these missing variables in language, literacy, and socialization, children of Color are thus seen as missing experiences and competence in connection with specific readiness "predictors" of literacy success in the preschool years and beyond.

PREDICTORS OF EARLY LITERACY SUCCESS AND ACHIEVEMENT

- receptive language skills
- productive language skills

- phonemic awareness
- rhyming
- concepts about print
- book knowledge
- sequencing
- background knowledge
- story recall

In light of these "missing" literacy variables, children of Color (and by association, their families) are seen as *starting from* and then continuing along a developmental trajectory of potential risk and failure without specific interventions and supports. This book addresses the overall goal of articulating a strength-based approach to literacy education that situates children of Color and their families within new narratives of literacy interest, achievement, and success.

Perspectives in the Book

I wrote this book in large part from my personal perspective and lived history as a Jewish/white individual and my professional experiences as a veteran teacher and teacher educator over the last 35 years. The book is written, then, in the vein and tradition of other white educators working with and writing about young children of Color. This book is also an accumulation of my thinking over many years about strength-based literacy education in preschool and is the product of my long-standing work in preschool and primary settings as a literacy teacher and teacher inquirer (Meier, 2000, 2004, 2009, 2011). The book is also based in part on my collaboration with other teacher inquirers, most recently at a preschool in San Francisco (Escamilla & Meier, 2017), and my work as a teacher educator teaching courses on multilingualism, multiliteracies, and teacher inquiry in early childhood education (Kroll & Meier, 2017; Meier & Henderson, 2007; Sisk-Hilton & Meier, 2016). Although I am a veteran literacy teacher, teacher inquirer, and teacher educator, I am also aware that I have certain blinders, biases, and preconceptions about the effectiveness of my own teaching, as well as the ease of transfer of my ideas and strategies to readers of this book. I have tried, then, to raise my awareness of my own biases and lack of expertise in certain areas of literacy education.

So to write an authentic and meaningful book on the literacy education of children of Color, I have also included the experiences and voices of a number of teachers, administrators, and families of Color whom I have known over many years in the San Francisco Bay area. I have relied on their perspectives to expand and deepen my own literacy ideas and experiences with children of Color, and to provide a well-rounded and sophisticated set of views on the literacy talents and abilities of young children of Color. I hope that I have accurately rendered their literacy experiences and perspectives, and that I have portrayed their hopes and dreams for their children and students with sensitivity and accuracy. There is no strength-based approach to children's literacy learning without an equally powerful strength-based approach founded upon the teaching and life talents of families and educators.

These early childhood teachers and leaders represent a range of years of experience from novice to veteran, and several are or were the parents of young children of Color in local public and independent preschools. The non-educator families are current or recent parents and grandparents of children aged three to five years who attend or attended local preschools. I spoke informally for about an hour with each educator and family member regarding their perspectives on the literacy talents, capabilities, and knowledge of young children of Color. I sent my discussion prompts to each family member or educator ahead of our conversation. Once I wrote up their comments and thoughts, I sent my writing to each educator and parent for their approval and possible editing.

In formulating the conversational prompts with the educators and families, I relied on aspects of narrative inquiry (Clandinin, 2013; Clandinin & Connelly, 2000; Lyons & LaBoskey, 2002; Sisk-Hilton & Meier, 2016), an approach that views "the landscape as narratively constructed" (Clandinin & Connelly, 2000, p. 2) and considers stories as critical for the formation of one's identity in and out of educational settings and institutions. I also employed elements of narrative-based interviewing (Boylorn, 2011; Seidman, 2013) as I wanted my conversations with the families and educators to feature the telling of memories, anecdotes, and stories about strength-based literacy teaching and learning.

KEY IDEA

Narrative inquiry emphasizes the use of story for articulating, sharing, and reflecting on important memories, experiences, and perspectives. It's a powerful form of professional inquiry and reflection for deepening our understanding of meaningful and effective literacy education.

I also wanted to take a reflexive stance (Bold, 2012) on my own literacy perspectives and practices, and to hold up the views and ideas of the family members and educators with whom I spoke as new mirrors for self-reflection and self-critique.

In our conversations, I relied on a basic set of conversational prompts, which I tweaked a bit as I spoke with the teachers and families and new directions for our conversations appeared.

For early childhood teachers, teaching assistants, and administrators:

- What do you see as the literacy talents, capabilities, and knowledge of young children of Color? Are there any specific examples that come to mind that illustrate these talents?
- As an educator of Color, are there particular feelings, ideas, experiences, or approaches that you draw upon to support the literacy learning of children of Color?
- Are there any particular theories, research, and/or policy that have most profoundly influenced your approach to literacy education?
- Are there any forms of practitioner inquiry and reflection that have raised your awareness of the literacy abilities of young children of Color and their families?
- What are the most effective literacy strategies (teaching or administrative) that you use in the classroom or at your school site for understanding and showcasing the literacy talents of young children of Color?

For families:

- What do you see as the literacy talents, capabilities, and knowledge of your child(ren)? Are there any specific examples that come to mind that illustrate these talents?
- Are there any particular experiences, events, hopes, or dreams that have most profoundly influenced your perspective?
- What are the most effective literacy strategies that you use at home and in the community for understanding and showcasing the literacy talents of your child(ren)?
- As a parent/grandparent/guardian of Color, are there specific goals, environments, materials, and/or strategies that you believe are most helpful for highlighting your child's/children's literacy talents in preschool settings?

I designed these prompts to stimulate conversation and to promote an exchange of perspectives on literacy based upon shared stories, examples, and experiences. I personally explained the purpose of the conversation and sent a copy of the prompts to each educator or family member before we spoke. I also encouraged each educator or family to ask me questions during our conversations.

Data Sources

In large part, the impetus for this book originated from my recent literacy teaching and inquiry work at three different preschools in the San Francisco Bay area. In the early years of my teaching career, I taught kindergarten and first grade at both independent and public schools, and then after I received my doctorate in education, I began working with children and their families in public pre-schools in the San Francisco Bay area. Over the last 25 years, in my capacity as a teacher educator in early childhood and elementary education, I have also worked with numerous teachers and leaders on creating, implementing, and reflecting on strength-based literacy education for children of Color and their families.

The examples and ideas that I present in this book from my teaching are relevant and applicable to a range of other preschool contexts that serve children of Color. This transfer of ideas and strategies, though, does not follow a direct line, as educators must do their own tinkering and adapting to fit local literacy traditions, needs, and goals. This tinkering and adaptation can be nurtured and supported by a professional interest in and devotion to the process of teacher inquiry, documentation, reflection, and change. The use of inquiry and reflection – collecting data on my teaching and the children's learning, and then reflecting on its meaning and value and making instructional changes – provides an intellectually engaging and socially conscious through-line for one's literacy intentions, beliefs, actions, and practices. I owe much of what I have learned about effective literacy education to a continuing passion for and systematic tinkering with key elements of inquiry, documentation, reflective practice, and educational change.

The teaching examples that I provide in this book are primarily based on three years of recent teaching at a local preschool in the San Francisco East Bay, which serves children of Color from surrounding neighborhoods. In Year 1, I worked as a part-time librarian at the preschool where I conducted whole-class read-alouds for three different classrooms of children aged three to five years. I also helped children select and exchange books on a weekly basis for the school's home-school bookbag program. In Years 2 and 3, Amanda Ibarra, the veteran and talented head teacher in one of the preschool classrooms, kindly accepted my offer to teach one morning a week and conduct whole-class read-alouds and small-group literacy activities. Over the course of three to five weeks, I cycled through small groups of the children and by year's end I had worked with all of the children. As the younger children stayed in Amanda's classroom for two to three years, I worked with approximately 40% of the same children during my two years in Amanda's classroom.

In this book, I present examples of my teaching and the children's learning from reviewing and reflecting on my teaching notes, children's conversations that I documented, audiotaped recordings of children's reading, and examples of the children's literacy products. I reviewed data from my library and teaching sessions over the course of three years, and looked for patterns and anomalies across this multi-year span both in my teaching and in the children's learning.

For the last eight years, I have also co-facilitated a teacher inquiry group of six teachers and two instructional coaches at Las Americas Children's Center, San Francisco Unified School District, which features two dual language (English/Spanish and English/Cantonese) classrooms and one Special Needs classroom. I also recently facilitated a short-term inquiry group of eight teachers at a Head

Start site in the San Francisco East Bay, a large preschool with ten classrooms. In presenting ideas and practices for using inquiry and reflection to understand and support the literacy talents of young children of Color, I relied on data from the inquiry group meetings at these two sites and my informal conversations with a number of the teachers.

The children featured in this book reflect the ethnic and economic, cultural, and linguistic mosaic of the three schools' immediate neighborhoods. The children include U.S.-born children of African descent as well as first- and second-generation immigrant families from Mexico, Central America, and Asia, and who attend both English-medium classrooms as well as dual language programs. Some of the children receive subsidized services, and their parents work as housekeepers, babysitters, cooks, painters, construction workers, and health care professionals and some attend classes to learn English and work toward a GED or college degree.

The Book's Organization – Themes and Chapters

In writing a book on such a large subject as a strength-based approach to the literacy learning of preschool children of Color, I emphasize three key themes to pull together the book's central purpose and message.

THE BOOK'S KEY THEMES

- Deepening Our Awareness (our personal and professional understanding of the literacy talents of children of Color)
- Achieving High Levels of Excellence (high levels of children's literacy learning and achievement as well as our own instructional goals and strategies)
- Increased Visibility (a depiction of children of Color as strong, agentic literacy learners, problem-solvers, and partners)

The first theme concerns determining our *awareness* of the need to reflect on how and why we perceive the literacy talents and abilities of children of Color and their families. It also involves expanding our awareness of where, how, and why we can make changes in our curriculum, learning environments, assessments, and teaching practices to strengthen our support of children's literacy talents and abilities.

The second theme concerns *excellence* and the need to recognize all children of Color as achieving at high levels of literacy engagement and learning according to their interests, talents, and resources. Excellence also recognizes children's literacy endeavors as essential to their development as successful learners, as scholars, and as carrying on the next generation of academic achievement for their schools, families, and communities.

The third theme focuses on *visibility* and the ways in which we can see children of Color as active, empowered learners in our classrooms, schools, and communities. A strength-based approach to literacy promotes an inclusive image of all children as visible in positive ways, contributing to their own learning, the learning of others, and communal literacy learning in the classroom and school. Visibility also recognizes the need to see ourselves as agentic educators who provide high-access and high-quality literacy learning during the preschool years. This also involves engagement with our colleagues, and the process of inquiry and reflection as a powerful form of professional growth and development for achieving new levels of dialogue and collaboration.

Section I, which includes Chapters 1–3, focuses on the theme of *deepening our awareness*. Chapter 1 defines and discusses key dimensions for conceptualizing a strength-based approach to the literacy learning of young children of Color, and cues the material to be covered in the book's upcoming chapters. This chapter provides a foundation of selected research and theory for the book's vision and pedagogical approach.

Chapter 2 examines the perspectives of families on the literacy learning of young children of Color both at home and at school. It is important for the voices and views of families of Color to be heard and accounted for in the formulation of a strength-based approach to literacy education.

Chapter 3 looks at the literacy perspectives and practices of a number of experienced and talented preschool teachers and administrators. This chapter broadens and deepens the theoretical foundation for the book as well as the perspectives of the families in Chapter 2.

Section II, which includes Chapters 4 and 5, examines the theme of *achieving high levels of excellence*. Chapter 4 helps us reconceptualize and implement child and culturally responsive children's literature and effective strategies to promote an early engagement with and understanding of reading texts. This is a practical chapter in which I provide examples that illustrate important ways that high-quality literature and reading strategies support children's literacy talents.

Chapter 5 discusses the aesthetic dimensions of art and dictation in children's literacy learning, and how these processes support the literacy interests and talents of children of Color. As another practical chapter, I provide examples of effective ways to conceptualize small-group literacy activities to promote strong connections to books, words, dictation, drawing, and early writing.

Section III, which includes Chapters 6 and 7, focuses on the theme of *increased visibility*. Chapter 6 examines the role of inquiry and reflection in providing a critical lens for improving literacy practices and understanding children's needs and talents. Inquiry is defined as the process whereby educators take an inquiry stance in their teaching and leadership, and integrate elements of data collection and analysis and reflection into their literacy teaching and leadership.

Chapter 7 discusses important next steps for maintaining and nurturing a strength-based approach to the literacy learning of children of Color. In this closing chapter, I offer a series of next steps for readers, for the field of early literacy education, and for a strength-based education for preschool children of Color.

Each chapter features an initial set of opening reflection prompts for readers; call-out boxes of key ideas, theory links, and quotes; and a concluding end-of-chapter set of reflection prompts. As much as possible, in each chapter's "theory links," I highlight relevant theories and approaches as discussed in Chapter 1.

In summary, this book examines the perspectives of educators and families regarding the literacy talents, abilities, and interests of preschool children of Color. The overall goal of this discussion is the conceptualization and implementation of high-access and high-quality literacy education for children of Color and their families. In doing so, I support *internal change* in ourselves as educators in how we can deepen our awareness of the literacy talents of children of Color, and *external change* for strengthening our literacy instruction and raising the visibility of the literacy achievement of children of Color in our classrooms, schools, communities, and within the early literacy field.

END-OF-CHAPTER REFLECTIONS

- What do you think of this chapter's discussion of "damage imagery," "blame-the-victim beliefs," and "blame-the-system beliefs" as linked with deficit views of the literacy talents and abilities of children of Color and their families?
- To what extent do the book's themes of deepening our awareness, high levels of excellence, and increased visibility resonate with you personally and professionally?
- Which ideas from this Introduction would you like to add to your own strength-based vision and philosophy of a strength-based approach to the literacy education of children of Color?
- Which ideas from this Introduction are you curious about, and which you would like to learn about further in the upcoming chapters?

References

Bold, C. (2012). *Using narrative in research*. London: SAGE.

Boylorn, R. (2011). Black kids' (B.K.) stories: Ta(l)king (about) race outside of the classroom. *Cultural Studies* < – > *Critical Methodologies, 11*(1), 59–70.

Clandinin, D. J. (2013). *Engaging in narrative inquiry*. Walnut Creek, CA: Left Coast Press.

Clandinin, D. J., & Connelly, F. M. (2000). *Narrative inquiry: Experience and story in qualitative research*. San Francisco, CA: Jossey-Bass.

Escamilla, I. M., & Meier, D. R. (2017). The promise of teacher inquiry and reflection: Early childhood teachers as change agents. *Studying Teacher Education, 14*(1), 1–19.

Hoover, M. E. R. (2005). Characteristics of Black schools at grade level revisited. In B. Hammond, M. E. R. Hoover, & I. P. McPhail (Eds.), *Teaching African American learners to read: Perspectives and practices* (pp. 66–78). Newark, DE: International Reading Association.

Kroll, L. K., & Meier, D. R. (2017). *Documentation and inquiry in the early childhood classroom: Research stories of engaged practitioners in urban centers and schools*. New York, NY: Routledge.

Lyons, N., & LaBoskey, V. (Eds.). (2002). *Narrative inquiry in practice: Advancing the knowledge of teaching*. New York, NY: Teachers College Press.

Meier, D. (2000). *Scribble scrabble: Learning to read and write – Success with diverse teachers, children, and families*. New York, NY: Teachers College Press.

Meier, D. (2004). *The young child's memory for words – First and second language and literacy*. New York, NY: Teachers College Press.

Meier, D. (Ed.). (2009). *Here's the story: Using narrative to promote children's language and literacy learning*. New York, NY: Teachers College Press.

Meier, D. (2011). *Teaching children to write: Constructing meaning and mastering mechanics*. (Co-Published). New York, NY: Teachers College Press. Berkeley, CA: National Writing Project.

Meier, D., & Henderson, B. (2007). *Learning from young children in the classroom: The art and science of teacher research*. New York, NY: Teachers College Press.

Seidman, I. (2013). *Interviewing as qualitative research* (4th ed.). New York, NY: Teachers College Press.

Sisk-Hilton, S., & Meier, D. R. (2016). *Narrative inquiry in early childhood and elementary school: Learning to teach, teaching well*. New York: Routledge.

Woodson, J. (2014). *Brown girl dreaming*. New York, NY: Penguin.

Wright, B. (2018). *The brilliance of Black boys: Cultivating school success in the early grades*. New York, NY: Teachers College Press.

Zirkel, S., & Johnson, T. (2016). Mirror, mirror on the wall: A critical examination of the conceptualization of the study of Black racial identity in education. *Educational Researcher, 45*(5), 301–311.

SECTION I
Deepening Our Awareness

1

A STRENGTH-BASED APPROACH TO PRESCHOOL LITERACY EDUCATION

OPENING REFLECTIONS

- What are key memories of your language and literacy learning at home, community, and school during your early childhood and elementary school years? For example, did you have experiences with oral stories and storytelling, conversation and dialogue, interactions with texts in religious or spiritual settings, art and dictation, singing and music, read-alouds, or book browsing?
- Which aspects of your language and literacy background and memories have you relied on to inform your educational philosophy about effective literacy teaching and learning?
- What are key ideas and approaches from your preservice and/or inservice professional development that focus or have focused on the language and literacy strengths of children of Color and their families?
- Which theoretical ideas and approaches have you found most valuable for conceptualizing a vision for strength-based literacy education?

Over the last 40 years, the field of early literacy education has shown an evolving understanding of the literacy capabilities of young children of Color, countering some but not all of the persistent deficit-based narratives in policy documents, curriculum, assessment, and preservice and service teacher training. Further, as resources are stretched thin in many public preschools, as we witness a revolving door of early childhood curricular changes and approaches and assessments, and endure high teacher and administrator turnover, we are at a critical juncture in the field of early childhood literacy education. We must now redouble our efforts to empower ourselves with the requisite knowledge base, pedagogical and instructional tools, and processes of reflection and inquiry to meet both old and new demands for high-quality early literacy instruction for children of Color and their families.

In this chapter, I tell a small story about the research, theoretical, and pedagogical literature that has most influenced my views on the literacy talents and abilities of children of Color. The discussion starts during the 1980s when I first started teaching young children and attended an M.A. program in education. It is a decade-by-decade story that I have witnessed and been part of as a graduate school student, teacher, teacher inquirer, teacher educator, and parent of two children.

In terms of the range of literature included in this chapter, I focus on theory and practice linking language, literacy, culture, and socialization most relevant to preschool as well as the primary grades. While this book focuses on the literacy learning of preschool children of Color, the literature discussion in this chapter provides a longer and broader historical and developmental view of a strength-based approach to literacy, and takes into account the continued policy emphasis on pushing down literacy goals and practices from the elementary school years into preschool literacy education. At certain points in this chapter, I also fast-forward the story and refer to how specific ideas or frameworks evolved and changed over time. I hope that by the end of this chapter, you will discover enough relevant theory and research for reconceptualizing and strengthening your own version of a strength-based approach to the literacy education of children of Color.

1980s – Language and Literacy Development and the Role of Socialization

In the mid-1980s, I earned my elementary school teaching credential, began teaching kindergarten and first grade, and completed on M.A. degree in reading and language. During this period of time, I was influenced by work in a number of areas of language and literacy development that provided me with a foundation in high-quality early literacy teaching, which specifically highlighted literacy as a sociocultural process and journey. The 1980s were a transitional decade in which more research began to consider what makes for effective literacy practices, along with a beginning examination of certain social, cultural, and discourse factors influencing children's literacy learning and socialization (Figure 1.1).

Jean Chall – Effective Early Reading Instruction

KEY IDEA

Effective reading instruction links attention to phonics, word structure, and word meaning within an engaging and yet structured instructional approach.

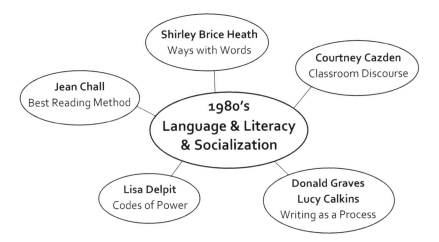

FIGURE 1.1 1980s – Influential Research and Theory

In my graduate school work at the M.A. level at the Harvard Graduate School of Education, I took courses with Jean Chall and I also tutored local elementary school students with reading challenges in the Harvard Reading Lab. At the time, Chall and others in the field of early reading research were continuing work started in earnest in the 1960s on providing a research base for the most effective instructional approach to early reading development. Chall examined the existing research literature on instructional methods that emphasized a meaning-based approach as well as those that highlighted a phonics and word analysis approach. In comparing these two dominant schools of thought on teaching early reading, Chall argued that while attention to meaning and comprehension are critical to learning to read (in fact, this process constitutes reading itself), over-attention to meaning meant that too many students do not learn the necessary skills and knowledge to decode text with fluency and efficiency. Chall also strongly advocated for the direct teaching of vocabulary in context, and I remember one day in the Reading Lab (which had two-way mirrors for observing our tutoring of local school children in need of reading support), when Chall came out from behind the two-way mirror and said to one of my fellow M.A.-level tutors, "What do you mean, you don't have time to teach vocabulary? You must!" The tutor was on the verge of tears, and from that day forward I have certainly remembered to incorporate vocabulary instruction into reading lessons!

Emergent Literacy

The idea of emergent literacy arose in the early 1980s partly in reaction to and against the reading readiness model, which certain researchers expanded upon from the work of Chall and others on phonics and structured reading instruction.

An emergent literacy approach emphasizes children's natural discovery of the forms and functions of written language. In this view, children do not learn to read and write based on a step-by-step model of learning a prescribed set of basic literacy skills. Rather, children are already reading and writing, though they are most likely not reading and writing in the conventional sense of decoding text or writing. For example, a four-year-old who memorizes stories and writes in scribbles is reading and writing in an emergent literacy perspective because she is engaged in meaningful ways with printed and written symbols.

In emergent literacy, children learn literacy as they come to it rather than as literacy comes to them, and children engage themselves and each other in meaningful and motivating experiences with sounds, letters, words, texts, and stories. Literacy instruction is therefore not contingent on a set or list of attributes or elements that children need to have in place before they are ready to learn to read and write. Children's engagement with books, reading, and writing is more holistic and organic as reading and writing activities are based upon children's natural sense of curiosity and discovery, and integrated into a classroom's overall curriculum and content.

Language Experience Approach

In the Language Experience Approach, children dictate a text or a story or a label for a drawing and an adult (or older child) writes down the child's language. The approach uses children's oral language talents and resources as a personal and social link to literacy. Starting with children's oral language, which is more sophisticated and complex in structure and content than their written language knowledge, we can extend and transfer it to writing and written language. This process of oral to written language is immediate and children can instantly see and hear the transformation of their spoken words onto the written page. It is an effective teaching strategy for many children, and greatly benefits new language learners (Gregory, 2008) who can begin their literacy learning on the basis of their oral language knowledge of additional languages. The approach can be used with whole-class, small-group, partner, and individual learning formats and groupings. In teaching small and large groups of children, language experience activities help us write down children's ideas and then revisit later for further exploration and discussion. For example, in Alonzo Williams's kindergarten class, the children dictated a text based on a recent field trip.

> We went to Hidden Villa Farm. We got on a big bus with t.v.'s. We drove on the freeway and counted the red cars and green signs. Then we ate snacks and looked at the animals. Then we went to go get some pumpkins. Then we ate lunch and played. We got back on the bus to go to school. The field trip was fun. The End

Alonzo displays this and other language experience products around his classroom so that "children can access the information."

Donald Graves and Lucy Calkins – Writing as a Process

Continuing the emphasis on linking oral language and children's emerging knowledge of written language conventions, other educators and researchers examined the writing development of young children during the early child-hood and elementary school years. In my M.A. courses and in professional devel-opment at the school where I taught first grade in the 1980s, the idea of teaching writing as a process captured the imagination and interest of an increasing num-ber of teachers. Expanding on earlier research and work on how young children learn to read through first experimenting with sound-symbol correspondence in their writing by Charles Read and Carol Chomsky and others, the writing-as-process advocates such as Donald Graves, Lucy Calkins, and Nancy Atwell argued that children learn to write when they follow the writing process of published authors. This work largely took place in primary grade classrooms in the Northeast and with children primarily from middle-class, Anglo European backgrounds.

The writing-as-process proponents proposed that children benefit from writ-ing about what they want to write, brainstorming topics and ideas on their own and with others, writing multiple drafts of their writing, conferring with peers and adults, and then publishing their writing and sharing their writing in public with varied audiences. This writing process, they argued, helps children internal-ize and appropriate the behaviors of what "real" writers do. The implications of this early work on writing as process for preschool literacy include the value of using oral language as a springboard for dictation and early writing, opportunities for structured social interaction and dialogue with peers and adults around writ-ten language, promoting children's identities as readers and writers, and gaining experience sharing one's literacy products with multiple audiences.

Lisa Delpit – Codes of Power

KEY IDEA

Codes of power refer to important and yet often hidden forms of language and literacy that students of Color must have direct and open access to for equitable literacy instruction and high academic achievement.

At the time, the most cogent and powerful critique of the writing process movement came from Lisa Delpit, who argued that the approach did not take into account the codes of power that undergird the academic achievement and school success of children of Color, whose talents and needs must be recognized and who often benefit from focused language and literacy goals and instructional practices. The codes of power refer to the implicit ways that mainstream, Anglo-European culture in the U.S. convey information about the most socially and academically valued forms and functions of literacy in formal school settings. Delpit argued that many children of Color are left out of the power structure and discourse forms that enable students to master the full range of literacy forms and functions that help students learn to read and write with accuracy, power, and persuasion.

If we fast-forward 25 years to current literacy pedagogies that affirm and support the literacy needs and talents of children of Color that I discuss later in this chapter, we can see the important historical role of Delpit's critique and challenge for literacy instruction to address the language, literacy, and social talents and needs of children of Color.

Courtney Cazden – Classroom Discourse

In an M.A. course that I took with Courtney Cazden, we examined the dominant forms and functions of classroom discourse that teachers and students use in classrooms to influence student success and achievement. I learned about the dominant participation patterns traditionally used in schools, and how these structures provide differential access for students from varied social, cultural, and linguistic groups to academic language, knowledge, and educational achievement. For example, most teachers use the I-R-E pattern of Initiating a prompt or question, then expecting a student Response, and then Evaluating that student's response, a pattern that often discourages extended peer-to-peer talk and emphasizes an expected correct answer from students. Other forms of classroom discourse, such as talk story from Hawai'i (Au, 1980), offer extended opportunities for students to discuss experiences and ideas relevant to learning important literacy forms and functions, which promotes more equitable and child-centered access to literacy learning and development.

KEY IDEA

A strength-based approach to literacy education avoids the I-R-E pattern of teacher initiation, student response, and teacher evaluation; instead it promotes more open-ended discussion and problem-solving via varied forms and functions of languages and literacies.

Shirley Brice Heath – Ways With Words

KEY IDEA

"Ways with words" refer to the language and literacy traditions that bind children with their siblings, with their classmates, and with adults in their homes and communities, and the nuanced ways that children are socialized into language and literacy patterns in their homes and communities.

In related work, education researchers and ethnographers such as Shirley Brice Heath looked deeply and widely at how young children are socialized into languages and literacies in home and community settings. Living near and working with children and families in the Piedmont Carolinas, Heath documented and examined the language and literacy perspectives and practices in three communities that varied by geography, race, class, culture, history, and language. Heath focused on "ways with words," which are the daily language and literacy traditions that connect children with their siblings, their classmates, and adults in their homes and communities. This socialization process, involving the moment-to-moment interactions, modeling, conversing, and teaching in which family and community members engage children constitutes powerful influences on how and why young children conceptualize and use oral and written languages. Further, Heath found that these patterns of socialization into language and literacy use influence children's differential access to school knowledge and learning. For instance, if children are not socialized into the dominant expectations and patterns of literacy use in schools, and teachers are not aware of these children's literacy talents and abilities, children are less likely to gain access to the dominant forms and functions of literacy in classrooms.

1990s – Culturally Responsive Teaching

My doctoral studies at the University of California at Berkeley in the early 1990s under the direction of Anne Haas Dyson extended my earlier knowledge of effective reading and writing instruction, classroom discourse, and early childhood socialization and language and literacy learning in and out of schools. Influential research and theory at the time helped me see deeper, more global influences underlying the literacy learning of young children of Color and their educational experiences and achievement in general (Figure 1.2).

FIGURE 1.2 1990s – Influential Research and Theory

Paulo Freire – Critical Pedagogy and Literacy Learning

Paulo Freire (1921–1997), the great Brazilian educator and thinker, articulated and shared his groundbreaking ideas on liberatory education and critical pedagogy on a global scale. Freire examined the large, macro-level divisions and disparities in the historical evolution of societies and educational systems that maintain divisive patterns of domination and oppression in societal and educational institutions. For example, in his early work teaching adult literacy with agricultural workers in rural Brazil, Freire used a generative pedagogy founded upon the workers' lived lives and the personal and cultural meanings they attached to words. Freire was interested in raising our consciousness as educators and as learners to promote a new vision and passion for education founded upon students' strengths, assets, and talents. His approach also emphasizes the honoring of humility and curiosity in teaching, the recognition of the social and cultural bonds between teachers and learners, and the need to take action and transform systemic educational inequality, racism, and disempowerment. While his work is surprisingly rarely cited in preschool literacy research and practice, Freire's ideas on generative teaching are a foundational piece for promoting a sense of agency and freedom in the literacy learning of young children of Color. For instance, later work by Vivian Vasquez and others on critical literacy highlights how young children can use language and literacy for challenging the status quo and promoting social justice and equity in classrooms and schools.

KEY IDEA

Paulo Freire's approach emphasizes the honoring of humility and curiosity in teaching, the recognition of the social and cultural bonds

> between teachers and learners, and the need to take action and trans-
> form systemic inequality, racism, and disempowerment in society and
> schools.

Luis Moll – Funds of Knowledge

The idea of funds of knowledge, first articulated by Luis Moll and colleagues, connects with Freire's emphasis on human dignity, assets, and education for freedom. Funds of knowledge refer to children's intimate knowledge of their daily lives in homes and communities – household chores and responsibilities, activities and relationships with relatives, friendships with peers, participation in religious institutions and traditions, and family places of work. Important current conceptualizations of an empowering literacy education advocate that children's community resources and home literacies make use of children's funds of knowledge to promote curricular access and student success. For example, when our early literacy curricula, environments, and interactions make room for children's funds of knowledge, for instance through home-school bookbag programs and encouraging children to talk, dictate, and create art about their families and communities, we encourage children to draw upon their expert knowledge.

KEY IDEA

> Funds of knowledge refer to children's intimate knowledge of their daily lives in homes and communities – household chores and responsibilities, activities and relationships with relatives, friendships with peers, participation in religious institutions and traditions, and family places of work.

Louise Derman-Sparks, Julie Olsen Edwards, and John Nimmo – Anti-Bias Education

Understanding, honoring, and designing literacy education that integrates children's funds of knowledge also promotes literacy education that features elements of anti-bias curriculum. In the work of Louise Derman-Sparks, Julie Olsen Edwards, John Nimmo, and others on anti-bias education, early childhood educators are asked to confront implicit and explicit biases and stereotypes to create anti-racist education that provides equitable access to school engagement and success. A commitment to anti-bias education helps promote children's positive social, racial, and cultural identity development; collaborative classroom communities; and socially just and inclusive learning environments for children and families of Color. One of the most significant contributions of an anti-bias approach is its emphasis on the selection of culturally, linguistically, and historically authentic learning environments and classroom materials. For instance, an emphasis on selecting and using high-quality multilingual and multicultural children's books beyond traditional Euro-centric books is a critical aspect of a strength-based approach to literacy.

Gloria Ladson-Billings and Geneva Gay – Culturally Responsive Education

Culturally responsive education, most powerfully articulated by Gloria Ladson-Billings, Geneva Gay, Lisa Delpit, and colleagues, is a broad and eclectic framework that focuses on culture, race, racism, and educational access and achievement. Important goals in this approach include (1) honoring and supporting children's cultural competence, or their culturally influenced knowledge and abilities, (2) emphasizing children's histories and identities as individuals and as members of multiple social and cultural communities, and (3) creating curriculum and classroom practices that support children's familiar and valued ways of understanding, interacting, talking, reading, and writing.

Culturally responsive education also speaks deeply to children's perceptions of what counts as accepted knowledge and successful learning in schools, and whose knowledge is worthy of attention in classrooms. Delpit (2008) exhorts us to make deep connections between literacy instruction, cultural and social identity, and children's attachment to classrooms and schooling.

> Finally, there is little in the curriculum that apprises the students of their intellectual legacy – of the fact that people who look like them created much of the knowledge base of today's world. When instruction is stripped of children's cultural legacies, then they are forced to believe that the world and all the good things in it were created by others. This leaves students further alienated from the school and its instructional goals, and more likely to view themselves as inadequate.
>
> *(p. 41)*

In current interpretations of culturally responsive education in early childhood by Mariana Souto-Manning and others, there is an emphasis on understanding how cultural traditions and practices within cultural groups shift and change over time. These researchers argue that this process requires a fluidity of awareness and action on the part of educators to support culturally relevant practices for children and families. Culturally influenced beliefs and practices are always changing and evolving to fit new social and educational contexts, and as educators we need to maintain a level of flexibility and ability to adapt cultural traditions and values with literacy goals, materials, and strategies.

Geneva Smitherman – African-American Language in Society and Education

A critical element of culturally responsive education is an understanding of how and why children of Color may speak and use a range of Englishes. For instance, African-American children benefit from increased teacher awareness of and skill in designing specific classroom structures and instructional strategies to honor their home and community language use. As the groundbreaking work of Geneva Smitherman and colleagues showed, African-American language is a structured, rule-governed form of expression, communication, thought, and cultural preservation and innovation. Smitherman argued that African-American language, in all its varied forms, is deserving of the same level of political and educational respect and legitimacy as more dominant forms of U.S. English. A strength-based literacy curriculum for children of African descent, then, integrates treasured and familiar modes of discourse and language in varied conversational formats, and the integration of oral stories, folktales, children's literature, and religious texts for African-American children and their families. These modes of language and literacy preservation and transmission, enacted in the myriad small interactions around oral and written language in classrooms, sustain and extend the linguistic histories and talents of African-American children and provide increased avenues to educational access and achievement.

Anne Haas Dyson – Children's Sociocultural Resources for Literacy Learning

Borrowing on ideas for linking social interaction, language, thought, and development from Lev Vygotsky and his Russian colleagues in the early 1900's, Anne Haas Dyson and others examined important intersections between children's social, cultural, linguistic, and literary worlds in classrooms. Dyson was my advisor in my doctoral studies, and had a formative influence on widening and deepening my understanding of expanded pathways to literacy engagement and achievement for young children of Color. In an effort to expand the pedagogical space for the range of linguistic and literary talents of young children of Color, Dyson argued that when young children are afforded learning opportunities for integrating what they know about the world, children tend to become more engaged and deepen their literacy engagement and development. These kinds of intentional, permeable boundaries for instruction and learning allow for a greater experimentation with and integration of children's emerging symbolization skills, their culturally influenced linguistic talents, and the multiple worlds of their drawn, written, dramatized, and digitized literacy work and play in classrooms.

> **KEY IDEA**
>
> Permeable boundaries in literacy education allow children to bring the full range of their social, cultural, and familial resources to bear on their literacy learning.

Vivian Paley – Play and Stories

An important element of this integration of childhood languages and literacies within classroom literacy instruction is also founded upon key forms and functions of story, storytelling, and story drama. As Vivian Paley (1929–2019) has shown in her kindergarten teaching and her books, story is the foundation for children's learning and development, especially when combined with children's play and social interactions. For Paley, teaching is the act of storying, and children and adults are all characters in the ever-evolving set of stories that we enact each year. Paley deeply believed that educators who integrate story and play promote opportunities for conversation, problem-solving, empathetic social interactions, quality oral language use, and a range of literary and art forms such as drama. The use of story, as envisioned by Paley and later interpreted by Gillian McNamee (2015) and others, also enables us to observe and document children's learning, interactions, and stories. This process of observation and documentation, based on stories told by teachers and children and read in books, deepens our ability to understand the important influences on children's learning and to self-reflect on needed changes in language and literacy curriculum, instructional strategies, and relationships with children and families.

2000s – Multilingualism and Multiliteracies

By the 2000s, new research looked at ways to understand and promote multilingualism and multiliteracies for an increasingly multilingual and transnational population of children and families (Figure 1.3). In reading through this literature, I have deepened and expanded my earlier doctoral-level knowledge of the relevant research through new ideas that emphasize the language and literacy talents, needs, and capabilities of young children of Color. The perspectives of a number of the educators and families that I feature in the next two chapters of this book are connected at deep levels with their hopes, dreams, and experiences with multilingualism, multiliteracies, culture, and the U.S. early childhood system.

Ofelia Garcia – Emergent Bilinguals

Influential research by Ofelia Garcia and colleagues has examined the language and literacy talents, interests, and needs of emergent bilinguals, and identified policies,

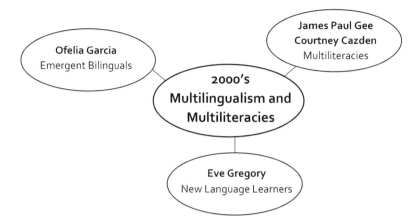

FIGURE 1.3   2000s – Influential Research and Theory

program structures, and strategies to support children's multilingual development. Garcia advocates for the conceptualization and integration of dynamic bilingualism as a way for young children and for teachers to capitalize and expand upon the varied forms and functions of the languages they speak, understand, and use. An important piece of this approach is the deep involvement of children's families and using their funds of knowledge as the basis for their multilingual participation in the social, cultural, and academic lives of their children. Dynamic bilingualism is also designed to promote equitable language and literacy instructional practices and opportunities for children to use their home languages as needed in classrooms to gain access to information, knowledge, and academic success.

To support children whose multilingual roots and traditions span borders and countries, Garcia and colleagues examine how transnational, emergent bilinguals have multilingual and multiliteracy talents and abilities that we must learn to recognize and make pedagogical space for in classrooms. These children and families may face unique challenges in adapting to new educational systems, curricular expectations, and language and literacy use. These children and youth might also travel back and forth across international borders to spend time with immediate and extended family members, and to communicate with family on a regular basis via smartphones and the Internet, which serve to preserve children's home languages and cultural ties.

Eve Gregory – New Language Learners

KEY IDEA

Mixed-aged interactions around literacy show evidence of synergy, a process whereby children engage in a complex set of interactions and

> multilingual/multiliteracy use and learn varied writing scripts, modes
> of text analysis, discourse, and interpretation.

Research by Eve Gregory, Charmian Kenner, and colleagues both in the U.K. and in the U.S. draw attention to the important role of families and communities in children's multilingual and multiliteracy learning. I spent some time in London visiting preschools where Gregory conducted her work, and saw first-hand the value of her research for documenting how intergenerational cultural traditions and views on literacy use in home and community influence children's school-based literacy learning.

Gregory and colleagues examined how collaborative extended family and community networks support children's social, cultural, and educational identities through joint attention to children's multilingual and multiliteracy growth. Gregory looked especially at students whom she called new language learners, who are children in the process of learning a second language and moving toward fluency and identification with multiple linguistic and cultural groups, communities, and cultures.

> [A new language learner] is a child who is at an early stage or who still lacks fluency in a second or additional language but whose ultimate aim is to become as fluent as possible, that is, able to communicate easily with others in the language and able positively to identify with both (or all if more than two are being learned) language groups and cultures.
>
> *(Gregory, 2008, p. 1)*

Gregory (2001) argues that children's "cultural knowledge" is influenced by experiences with literacy in homes and communities, and through the particular socially and cognitively based strategies that children and adults engage in together. For example, in looking at children's play and literacy use in "informal" learning situations such as in children's homes and communities, Gregory (2001) looked "beyond existing metaphors of 'scaffolding,' 'guided participation' or 'collaborative learning' to explain the reciprocity that might be taking place between young siblings" (p. 305). Gregory emphasizes the power of "synergy, a unique reciprocity whereby siblings act as adjuvants in each other's learning" (p. 309), and older children teach younger children and thereby increase their own literacy learning. In this process of synergy, siblings engage in "cultural routines" around literacy that provide a complex and influential set of interactions using oral and nonverbal language.

Gregory's ideas for supporting the literacy learning of new language learners were in part built upon research by James Paul Gee, The New London Group, and others arguing for a greater valuing of the range of literacies that children bring to school. Gregory and colleagues also borrowed ideas from Vygotsky (1978) on language and literacy learning as a sociocultural process, and examined how varied adults, children, and youth play important roles in young children's multilingual learning. For instance, in her work in London, Gregory (1998) looked at how Bengali-origin grandparents and older siblings play a pivotal role in helping their young grandchildren in their language and literacy associated with studying the Qur'an in community-based educational settings. Gregory argues that these mixed-aged interactions show evidence of synergy, a process whereby children engage in a complex set of interactions and multilingual/multiliteracy use and learn varied writing scripts, modes of text analysis, discourse, and interpretation.

Gregory is also interested in the interrelationships between cultures, codes, and contexts in the literacy learning of new language learners. Borrowing on Vygotskian and other sociocultural perspectives, Gregory emphasizes the theoretical and practical power of two frameworks: the inside-out and the outside-in approaches. In the inside-out approach, literacy instruction "starts from the child's own knowledge and experience and gradually moves outwards into the new world; it starts from the smallest units of meaning, the letters and words, and gradually links these into complete texts" (2008, p. 160). Gregory notes that the inside-out approach is not only based on children's known experiences but also includes the range of new and future literacy experiences and knowledge that are to come.

The outside-in approach utilizes stories and narrative. It emphasizes story structure, story language, chunking of story language, sociomoral aspects of stories, and semantic, syntactic, bibliographic, lexical and grapho-phonic literacy clues (p. 184). The outside-in approach also offers new language learners "the process of initiation into a new culture" (p. 186), and this process becomes even "more meaningful" through "first-hand experiences" with literacy and other activities. Gregory argues for the ultimate goal of integrating the inside-out and outside-in approaches to literacy to promote rich and long-lasting learning for new language learners.

2010s – Educational Change and Professional Development

In this last section, I highlight selected recent approaches that deepen our passion for personal change and professional transformation through increased attention to self-reflection, collaborative inquiry and dialogue, and our professional identities as change agents (Figure 1.4).

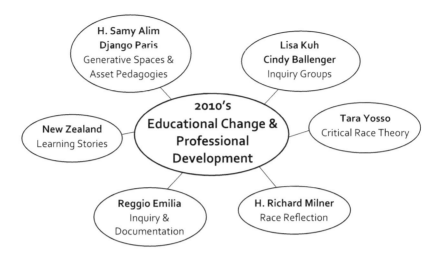

FIGURE 1.4   2010s – Influential Research and Theory

Tara Yosso and Daniel Solórzano – Critical Race Theory

> **KEY IDEA**
>
> Critical race theory examines the educational disparities in society and education as connected with societal, institutional, and personal racism and discrimination.

Tara Yosso, Daniel Solórzano, and others have looked at how historical and societal racism continues to influence the quality of our relationships with children and families, our perceptions of the literacy talents and abilities of children of Color, and our literacy philosophies and teaching practices. Critical race theory examines the educational disparities in society and education as connected with societal, institutional, and personal racism and discrimination. The framework challenges us to consider how racism in educational institutions and policies continues to inhibit access for children of Color and their families to social, human, cultural, educational, and navigational capital necessary for school success and achievement. The framework can help us consider how systemic racism and exclusionary practices and policies marginalize and disempower children of Color and their families from high-access, high-quality preschools and literacy education. For example, the approach can also challenge us to reflect on the implications of certain preschool assessments, which can contribute to a fragmented literacy curriculum for children of Color, hampering teachers' efforts to support a comprehensive, strength-based approach to children's literacy development.

H. Samy Alim, Django Paris, and H. Richard Milner – Generative Spaces, Asset Pedagogies, and Race Reflection

KEY IDEA

The frameworks of generative spaces, asset pedagogies, and race reflection encourage us to engage in the external process of examining deficit aspects of literacy policies, curricula, and practices as well as the internal process of critical reflexivity to re-voice persistent forms of racism and other -isms in the pursuit of strength-based literacy education.

The frameworks of generative spaces and asset pedagogies, articulated by H. Samy Alim, Django Paris, and others, and race reflection by H. Richard Milner, also raise our awareness of how a strength-based approach to literacy education must be founded upon children's cultural competencies and literacy interests, talents, abilities, and knowledge. These frameworks encourage us to engage in the external process of examining deficit aspects of literacy policies, curricula, and practices as well as the internal process of critical reflexivity to re-voice persistent forms of racism and other -isms in the pursuit of high-access, high-quality literacy education. This process of looking at our perceptions helps us successfully address the all-important early stage of reframing from categorizing children by preconceived standards and expectations, and to take the next step to recognize and honor important elements of children's sociocultural histories and talents. In the process of race reflection, personal and professional reflection is a powerful vehicle for rethinking literacy education and showcasing the social, cultural, educational, and literacy talents and interests of children of Color. In this inquiry-based process, race reflection aims to help us see children as whole individuals rather than as fragmented learners, and to recognize how our biases and perceptions might impede the literacy learning and achievement of children of Color.

We can build upon our knowledge of and skill in understanding generative spaces, asset pedagogies, and race reflection with a deep personal and institutional commitment to professional inquiry, documentation, and inquiry. This is an organized and collaborative process in which educators (and children and families can serve as co-researchers) observe, collect, and document classroom learning, represent the key findings and lessons learned, share these findings with each other, and work together for educational change based upon their documentation and reflection. The adoption and nurturing of inquiry and reflection in preschools can help educators find the critical ideas and lenses for understanding and improving literacy goals and practices for themselves, their students, and their families.

Reggio Emilia, Italy – Languages, Inquiry, and Documentation

KEY IDEA

The use of inquiry, documentation, and reflection is a systematic process in which educators (and with children and families as potential co-researchers) observe, collect, and document classroom learning for the goal of social, educational, and political change. In the Reggio Emilia view of a pedagogy of listening, educators use documentation and reflection to join children where they are in their literacy learning and attune their teaching to the inner workings of children's hearts, minds, bodies, languages, and literacies.

We owe much of our current understanding of high-quality inquiry, documentation, and reflection to the work of Loris Malaguzzi, Carlina Rinaldi, and their Reggio Emilia colleagues. These educators have argued for a number of years that a strength-based approach to education is founded upon cultivating a lifelong belief in the value of observation, documentation, reflection, and dialogue. Reggio educators believe that this process elevates the image of young children as highly capable problem-solvers, thinkers, and social, cultural, and intellectual actors. The Reggio approach is founded upon the careful collection and documentation of children's learning, which provides a permanent record of critical moments, objects, experiences, discoveries, and tensions in children's learning. In this empowering perspective, teachers and children and families take on agentic roles in education in and out of school, and in a pedagogy of listening, educators join children where they are in their literacy learning and attune their teaching to the inner workings of children's hearts, minds, bodies, languages, and literacies. This process allows for a finely tuned approach to observation and documentation in classrooms that also supports the affective, social, moral, and political dimensions of teaching and learning for teachers, children, and families.

The process of inquiry and reflection also provides a valuable structure for professional collaboration and dialogue to focus on multilingual and multiliteracy learning, relationships with families, and authentic assessment. In my current work with teachers, coaches, and leaders around inquiry and reflection, I continue to witness the power of the Reggio approach to the inquiry and reflection process for bringing educators together for collaborative investigation, question-posing, dialogue, sharing, and personal and professional transformation. It remains an importance international influence for creating local, home-grown change in how we conceptualize and implement literacy instruction in our local contexts.

New Zealand – Learning Stories

KEY IDEA

Learning stories are an authentic form of assessment that use text and visuals to capture key moments in children's learning and promote a strength-based portrait of the talents and abilities of young children and their families.

New Zealand educators such as Margaret Carr, Lesley Pohio, Adrienne Samsom, and others emphasize the value of the national New Zealand curriculum of *Te Whāriki* and the use of learning stories for promoting documentation, reflection, and educational equity and social justice. In the *Te Whāriki* curriculum, the beliefs and traditions of the indigenous Māori people are at the foundation of the curriculum's policies, philosophy, teaching practices, assessments, and family involvement. The curriculum recognizes the deep historical need and value of indigenous approaches to languages, literacies, culture, the arts, and the natural environment. This strength-based approach to early childhood also privileges culturally responsive forms and functions of story, and uses stories told, enacted, photographed, and written by children, teachers, and families as important modes of authentic assessment, reflection, educational change, and family and community involvement. In the learning stories approach, teachers engage in a continual process of observation, documentation, and the creation of stories about the the learning of individual and small groups of children that feature written text, photographs, and responses from children's families.

U.S. Contexts – Inquiry Groups

KEY IDEA

Inquiry groups provide a regular, structured professional forum for early childhood teachers, coaches, administrators, and other professionals to present and discuss documentation and to reflect on next steps for inquiry, teaching, and leadership.

In U.S. early childhood contexts, the work of Shareen Abramson, Cindy Ballenger, Barbara Henderson, Linda Kroll, Lisa Kuh, Ben Mardell, Andrew Stremmel, and others demonstrate how the creation of inquiry groups provides a forum for sharing documentation and promoting professional dialogue and communication. The heart of teacher inquiry and reflection involves teachers collecting data and documenting their teaching and interactions with children and families, as well as children's learning and engagement. In collaborative inquiry groups, teachers bring their documentation in the form of photographs, video and audio clips, stories, panels, and books to present and share with colleagues. The documentation presented with and to colleagues can be in-process or more complete and polished as fits the inquiry journey for the teacher inquirers.

Inquiry groups provide a rich and engaging professional forum for the exchange of insights into strength-based teaching and learning for children of Color and their families. They are an effective professional forum for showcasing the multilingual and multiliteracy talents and abilities of children, and their families, as well as early childhood educators themselves. The process supports teachers as engaged, critical educators who are adept at documentation and analysis, and as highly capable inquirers eager to share and reflect with colleagues and outside audiences. I have found that inquiry groups, once created and nurtured over the long-term, often organically expand to include instructional coaches, administrators, families, and outside professionals, and the group's documentation can be shared locally and more broadly via electronic platforms and other means.

Chapter Summary

In this chapter, I have told a brief story of some of the most influential research and theory that has influenced my vision for a strength-based approach to the literacy education for young children of Color. In writing this chapter, I had the chance to revisit key people, ideas, theories, and approaches that I now more clearly see as essential for understanding and supporting the literacy talents of preschool children of Color. In telling this story, I also see more clearly the work that we have ahead of us in preschool literacy education – selecting those ideas and theories that we are passionate about, putting them into practice, and reflecting on ways to improve and deepen our literacy teaching over time with colleagues. To do this deep and meaningful literacy work, it is helpful for us to adopt and adapt the goals and tools of inquiry, documentation, and reflection to promote new levels of professional collaboration and dialogue.

In the next chapter, I examine the perspectives of several families of Color concerning their children's literacy talents, interests, and abilities. As you read the next chapter, please keep in mind the important theories and practices from this first chapter as we consider the literacy hopes, dreams, and experiences of families of Color.

END-OF-CHAPTER REFLECTIONS

- Which theories and approaches did you find most useful for deepening and expanding your conceptual understanding of a strength-based approach to literacy education for children of Color and their families?
- How do these ideas and approaches support and extend your instructional goals and strategies?
- Which areas would you like to learn more about? Please see the useful resources at the end of this chapter, which include the material cited in this chapter as well as additional resources. Note those articles and books that look particularly promising for your further reading and reflection.

Useful Resources

Literacy Development, Socialization, and Discourse

Au, K. H. P. (1980). Participation structures in a reading lesson with Hawaiian children: Analysis of a culturally appropriate instructional event. *Anthropology & Education Quarterly*, *11*(2), 91–115.

Au, K. H. P. (1993). *Literacy instruction in multicultural settings*. New York, NY: Wadsworth Publishing Company.

Cazden, C. (2001). *Classroom discourse: The language of teaching and learning* (2nd ed.). Portsmouth, NH: Heinemann Educational Books.

Derman-Sparks, L. (1989). *Anti-bias curriculum: Tools for empowering young children*. Washington, DC: National Association for the Education of Young Children.

Derman-Sparks, L., & Edwards, J. O. (2010). *Anti-bias education for young children and ourselves*. Washington, DC: NAEYC.

Derman-Sparks, L., LeeKeenan, D., & Nimmo, J. (2014). *Leading anti-bias early childhood programs: A guide for change*. New York, NY: Teachers College Press.

Dyson, A. H. (2016). *Negotiating a permeable curriculum: On literacy, diversity, and the interplay of children's and teachers' worlds* (B. Kabuto, Ed.). New York, NY: Garn Press.

Gardner-Neblett, N., Pungello, E. P., & Iruka, I. U. (2012). Oral narrative skills: Implications for the reading development of African American children. *Child Development Perspectives*, *6*(3), 218–224.

Genishi, C., & Dyson, A. H. (2015). *Children, language, and literacy: Diverse learners in diverse times*. New York, NY: Teachers College Press.

Giudici, C. (2011). The enchantment of writing. *Innovations in Early Education: The International Reggio Exchange, 18*(2), 12–20.

Heath, S. B. (1983). *Ways with words: Language, life and work in communities and classrooms.* Cambridge: Cambridge University Press.

Iruka, I. U., Gardner-Neblett, N., Matthews, J. S., & Winn, D. M. C. (2014). Preschool to kindergarten transition patterns for African American boys. *Early Childhood Research Quarterly, 29*(2), 106–117.

Kliewer, C., Fitzgerald, L. M., Meyer-Mork, J., Hartman, P., English-Sand, P., & Raschke, D. (2004). Citizenship for all in the literate community: An ethnography of young children with significant disabilities in inclusive early childhood settings. *Harvard Educational Review, 74*(4), 373–403.

McNamee, G. (2015). *The high-performing preschool: Story-acting in Head Start classrooms.* Chicago, IL: University of Chicago Press.

Meier, D. (2000). *Scribble scrabble: Learning to read and write – Success with diverse teachers, children, and families.* New York, NY: Teachers College Press.

Vygotsky, L. S. (1978). *Mind in society.* Cambridge, MA: Harvard University Press.

Culturally Responsive Education

Ballenger, C. (1999). *Teaching other people's children: Literacy and learning in a bilingual classroom.* New York, NY: Teachers College Press.

Banks, J. A. (1994). *An introduction to multicultural education.* Needham Heights, MA: Allyn and Bacon.

Clark, E. R., Flores, B. B., Smith, H. L., & Gonzalez, D. A. (2016). *Multicultural literature for Latino bilingual children: Their words, their worlds.* New York, NY: Rowman & Littlefield.

Colegrove, K. S. S., & Adair, J. K. (2014). Countering deficit thinking: Agency, capabilities and the early learning experiences of children of Latina/o immigrants. *Contemporary Issues in Early Childhood, 15*(2), 122–135.

Compton-Lilly, C. (2010). *Breaking the silence: Recognizing the social and cultural resources students bring to the classroom.* Newark, DE: International Reading Association.

Delpit, L. (2006). *Other people's children: Cultural conflict in the classroom.* New York, NY: The New Press.

Delpit, L., & Dowdy, J. K. (Eds.). (2008). *The skin that we speak: Thoughts on language and culture in the classroom.* New York: The New Press.

Emden, C. (2006). *For White folks who teach in the hood . . . and the rest of y'all too: Reality pedagogy and urban education.* Boston, MA: Beacon Press.

Freire, P. (1996). *Pedagogy of the oppressed (revised).* New York, NY: Continuum.

Freire, P. (2006). Cultural action and conscientization. In B. Piper, S. Dryden-Peterson, & Y. S. Kim (Eds.), *International education for the millennium: Toward access, equity, and quality: Harvard educational review reprint series* (pp. 55–74). Cambridge, MA: Harvard Education Press.

Freire, P., & Macedo, D. (1995). A dialogue: Culture, language, and race. *Harvard Educational Review, 65*(3), 377–403.

Gallo, S. (2017). *Mi padre: Mexican immigrant fathers and their children's education.* New York, NY: Teachers College Press.

Gay, G. (1995). Bridging multicultural theory and practice. *Multicultural Education, 3*(1), 4–9.

Gay, G. (2018). *Culturally responsive teaching: Theory, research, and practice.* New York, NY: Teachers College Press.

González, N., Moll, L. C., & Amanti, C. (Eds.). (2006). *Funds of knowledge: Theorizing practices in households, communities, and classrooms.* New York, NY: Routledge.

Helmberger, J. (2011). Representing cultural identity in children's literature: Black children in their communities. In V. Yenika-Agbaw & M. Napoli (Eds.), *African and African American children's and adolescent literature in the classroom: A critical guide: Black studies and critical thinking* (Vol. 11, pp. 33–44). New York, NY: Peter Lang.

Hoover, M. E. R. (2005). Characteristics of Black schools at grade level revisited. In B. Hammond, M. E. R. Hoover, & I. P. McPhail (Eds.), *Teaching African American learners to read: Perspectives and practices* (pp. 66–78). Newark, DE: International Reading Association.

Howard, T. (2008). Who really cares? The disenfranchisement of African American males in PreK-12 schools: A critical race theory perspective. *Teachers College Record, 110*(5), 954–985.

Howard, T. C., & Rodriguez-Scheel, A. (2017). Culturally relevant pedagogy 20 years later: Progress or pontificating? What have we learned, and where do we go? *Teachers College Record, 119*(1), n1.

Kuby, C. R. (2013). *Critical literacy in the early childhood classroom: Unpacking histories, unlearning privilege.* New York, NY: Teachers College Press.

Ladson-Billings, G. (1995). Culturally relevant teaching. *Theory Into Practice, 34*(3), 150-151.

Ladson-Billings, G. (2008). I ain't writin' nuttin': Permissions to fail and demands to succeed in urban classrooms. In L. Delpit & J. K. Dowdy (Eds.), *The skin that we speak: Thoughts on language and culture in the classroom* (pp. 107–120). New York, NY: The New Press.

Ladson-Billings, G. (2009). *The dreamkeepers: Successful teachers of African American children.* San Francisco, CA: Jossey-Bass.

Ladson-Billings, G. (2014). Culturally relevant pedagogy 2.0: Aka the remix. *Harvard Educational Review, 84*(1), 74–84.

Moll, L. C., Amanti, C., Neff, D., & Gonzalez, N. (1992). Funds of knowledge for teaching: Using a qualitative approach to connect homes and classrooms. *Theory Into Practice, 31*(2), 132–141.

Moore, R. (1998). *Investigating culturally engaged instruction: A report to the Spencer Foundation.* Chicago, IL: Spencer Foundation.

Wright, B. L., & Counsell, S. L. (2018). *The brilliance of Black boys: Cultivating school success in the early grades.* New York, NY: Teachers College Press.

Zirkel, S., & Johnson, T. (2016). Mirror, mirror on the wall: A critical examination of the conceptualization of the study of Black racial identity in education. *Educational Researcher, 45*(5), 301–311.

Multilingualism and Multiliteracies

Barrett, R. (2014). You are what you speak: Language variation, identity, and education. In A. Y. Young, R. Barrett, Y. Young-Rivera, & K. M. Lovejoy (Eds.), *Other people's English: Code-meshing, code-switching, and African American literacy* (pp. 24–32). New York, NY: Teachers College Press.

Campano, G., Ghiso, M. P., & Welch, B. J. (2016). *Partnering with immigrant communities: Action through literacy.* New York, NY: Teachers College Press.

Delpit, L. (1986). Skills and other dilemmas of a progressive black educator. *Harvard Educational Review, 56*(4), 379–386.

Delpit, L. (2008). No kinda sense. In L. Delpit & J. K. Dowdy (Eds.), *The skin that we speak: Thoughts on language and culture in the classroom* (pp. 31–48). New York, NY: The New Press.

Garcia, O., Kleifgen, J. A., & Falchi, L. (2008). From English language learners to emergent bilinguals. *Equity Matters: Research Review, 1,* 1–9.

Gee, J. P. (2015). *Social linguistics and literacies: Ideology in discourses* (5th ed.). London: Routledge/Falmer.

Gregory, E. (1998). Siblings as mediators of literacy in linguistic minority communities. *Language and Education, 12*(1), 33–54.

Gregory, E. (2001). Sisters and brothers as language and literacy teachers: Synergy between siblings playing and working together. *Journal of Early Childhood Literacy, 1*(3), 301–322.

Gregory, E. (2008). *Learning to read in a new language: Making sense of words and worlds.* London: Sage.

Gregory, E., Long, S., & Volk, D. (Eds.). (2004). *Many pathways to literacy: Young children learning with siblings, grandparents, peers, and communities.* Hove, UK: Psychology Press.

Gregory, E., & Williams, A. (2000). *City literacies: Learning to read across generations and cultures.* Hove, UK: Psychology Press.

Kenner, C. (2004). *Becoming biliterate: Young children learning different writing systems.* Stoke-on-Trent, UK: Trentham.

Kenner, C., Ruby, M., Jessel, J., Gregory, E., & Arju, T. (2007). Intergenerational learning between children and grandparents in East London. *Journal of Early Childhood Research, 5*(3), 219–243.

Lewis, T. Y. (2009). *Family literacy and digital literacies: A redefined approach to examining social practices of an African-American family* (unpublished doctoral dissertation). State University of New York, Albany.

Lewis, T. Y. (2013). "We txt 2 sty cnnectd:" An African American mother and son communicate: Digital literacies, meaning-making, and activity theory systems. *Journal of Education, 193*(2), 1–13.

Lewis Ellison, T., & Wang, H. (2018). Resisting and redirecting: Agentive practices within an African American parent –Child dyad during digital storytelling. *Journal of Literacy Research, 50*(1), 52–73.

Lytra, V., Volk, D., & Gregory, E. (Eds.). (2016). *Navigating languages, literacies and identities: Religion in young lives.* New York, NY: Routledge.

Martínez-Álvarez, P., & Ghiso, M. P. (2012). Creative literacies and learning with Latino emergent bilinguals. *LEARNing Landscapes, 6*(1), 273–296.

The New London Group. (1996). A pedagogy of multiliteracies: Designing social futures. *Harvard Educational Review, 66*(1), 60–93.

Orellana, M. F. (2009). *Translating childhoods: Immigrant youth, language, and culture.* New Brunswick, NJ: Rutgers University Press.

Orellana, M. F., Thorne, B., Chee, A., & Lam, W. S. E. (2001). Transnational childhoods: The participation of children in processes of family migration. *Social Problems, 48*(4), 572–591.

Smitherman, G. (2006). *Word from the mother: Language and African Americans.* New York, NY: Routledge.

Souto-Manning, M. (2016). Honoring and building on the rich literacy practices of young bilingual and multilingual learners. *The Reading Teacher, 70*(3), 263–271.

Stockman, I. (2010). A review of developmental and applied language research on African American children: From a deficit to difference perspective on dialect differences. *Language, Speech, and Hearing in Schools, 41,* 23–38.

US Department of Health and Human Services. (2016). *Policy statement on supporting the development of children who are dual language learners in early childhood programs*. ERIC Clearinghouse.

Vasquez, V. M. (2004). *Negotiating critical literacies with young children*. Mahwah, NJ: Lawrence Erlbaum.

Vasquez, V. M. (2017). Critical literacy. *Oxford Research Encyclopedia of Education*. doi:10.1093/acrefore/9780190264093.013.20

Yenika-Agbaw, V., & Napoli, M. (Eds.). (2011). *African and African American children's and adolescent literature in the classroom: A critical guide: Black studies and critical thinking* (Vol. 11, pp. 33-44). New York, NY: Peter Lang.

Inquiry, Professional Development, and Educational Change

Brookline Teacher Research Seminar & Ballenger. (2003). *Regarding children's words: Teacher research on language and literacy*. New York, NY: Teachers College Press.

Campano, G. (2009). Teacher research as a collective struggle for humanization. In *Inquiry as stance: Practitioner research for the next generation* (pp. 326-341). New York, NY: Teachers College Press.

Edwards, C., & Rinaldi, C. (Eds.). (2009). *The diary of Laura: Perspectives on a Reggio Emilia diary*. St. Paul, MN: Red Leaf Press.

Escamilla, I. M., & Meier, D. R. (2017). The promise of teacher inquiry and reflection: Early childhood teachers as change agents. *Studying Teacher Education, 14*(1), 1–19.

Goeson, R. (2014). Finding our voices through narrative inquiry: Exploring a conflict of cultures. *Voices of Practitioners, 9*(1), 1–22.

Johanson, S., & Kuh, L. (2013). Critical friends groups in an early childhood setting: Building a culture of collaboration. *Voices of Practitioners, 8*(2), 1–16.

Kroll, L. K., & Meier, D. R. (2017). *Documentation and inquiry in the early childhood classroom: Research stories of engaged practitioners in urban centers and schools*. New York, NY: Routledge.

Mardell, B., LeeKeenan, D., Given, H., Robinson, D., Merino, B., & Liu-Constant, Y. (2009). Zooms: Promoting school wide inquiry and improving practice. *Voices of Practitioners, 4*(1), 1–15.

Milner, H. R. (2003). Teacher reflection and race in cultural contexts: History, meanings, and methods in teaching. *Theory Into Practice, 42*(3), 173–180.

Milner, H. R. (2007). Race, culture, and researcher positionality: Working through dangers seen, unseen, and unforeseen. *Educational Researcher, 36*(7), 388–400.

Paley, V. G. (1998). *The girl with the brown crayon*. Cambridge, MA: Harvard University Press.

Paley, V. P. (1981). *Wally's stories*. Cambridge, MA: Harvard University Press.

Paris, D., & Alim, H. S. (2014). What are we seeking to sustain through culturally sustaining pedagogy? A loving critique forward. *Harvard Educational Review, 84*(1), 85–100.

Paris, D., & Alim, H. S. (Eds.). (2017). *Culturally sustaining pedagogies: Teaching and learning for justice in a changing world*. New York, NY: Teachers College Press.

Rust, F. (2009). Teacher research and the problem of practice. *Teachers College Record, 111*(8), 1882–1893.

Sisk-Hilton, S., & Meier, D. R. (2016). *Narrative inquiry in early childhood and elementary school: Learning to teach, teaching well*. New York, NY: Routledge.

Solórzano, D. G., & Yosso, T. J. (2002). Critical race methodology: Counter-storytelling as an analytical framework for education research. *Qualitative Inquiry, 8*(1), 23–44.

Souto-Manning, M. (2006). A Latina teacher's journal: Reflections on language, culture, literacy, and discourse practices. *Journal of Latinos and Education, 5*(4), 293–304.

Souto-Manning, M. (2013). *Multicultural teaching in the early childhood classroom: Approaches, strategies, and tools, preschool-2nd grade.* New York, NY: Teachers College Press.

Souto-Manning, M., & Martell, J. (2016). *Reading, writing, and talk: Inclusive teaching strategies for diverse learners, K-2.* New York, NY: Teachers College Press.

Stremmel, A. (2014). The power of narrative inquiry to transform both teacher and mentor. *Voices of Practitioners, 9*(1), 1–5.

Wilson, P. H., Sztajn, P., Edgington, C., Webb, J., & Myers, M. (2017). Changes in teachers' discourse about students in a professional development on learning trajectories. *American Educational Research Journal, 54*(3), 568–604.

Yosso, T. J. (2005). Whose culture has capital? A critical race theory discussion of community cultural wealth. *Race Ethnicity and Education, 8*(1), 69–91.

2

FAMILY PERSPECTIVES ON LITERACY LEARNING – ASPIRATIONS, CHALLENGES, AND PRACTICES

OPENING REFLECTIONS

- What personal literacy values and beliefs have you held onto since your childhood and youth that you still value today in working with families around literacy education?
- How has your professional preservice and inservice education influenced your perspective on the literacy talents and strengths of families of Color?
- Which aspects of your literacy work with families do you see as your strengths?
- What are a few key goals for deepening your literacy work and relationships with families? Which of these goals are short-term and which are more long-term?

Based upon the research and practice that I presented in Chapter 1, a strength-based perspective on the literacy learning of children of Color is supported and guided by the values, beliefs, and practices of children, families, communities, and educators. In this chapter, I present the perspectives of several parents of Color regarding their children's literacy talents, and show the human side of families' expectations, hopes, and dreams for their children's literacy learning. In discussing their perspectives, I emphasize their aspirations for their children's literacy achievement, the challenges that they face in promoting their children's literacy at home and school, and the literacy practices that they enact at home.

KEY IDEA

- Literacy Aspirations = hopes and dreams based on family and cultural values
- Literacy Challenges = educational and societal barriers to literacy learning and achievement
- Literacy Practices = Literacy-related goals, materials, and strategies at home and in the community

---

Deepening our knowledge of the goals and expectations of families of Color for their children's literacy learning strengthens our conceptualization and implementation of a strength-based literacy philosophy and set of practices. It provides a more nuanced, sensitive approach to literacy that accounts for family goals, strengths, challenges, dilemmas, and practices (Figure 2.1). It is also helpful to know how families view their own roles in their children's literacy success, and to find new ways to see families as articulate, agentic actors committed to their children's literacy education at home and school.

My understanding of the literacy perspectives of families of Color was broadened and deepened in these conversations with the families. I learned anew about the hopes, dreams, and aspirations that families have for their children, and also for themselves as carriers of familial, historical, and cultural traditions and values. Some of their perspectives also challenged me to question my own training and work as a teacher educator that has largely been influenced by an emphasis on early childhood play, self-discovery, and open-ended language and literacy activities. The families showed me new possibilities for melding elements of play and

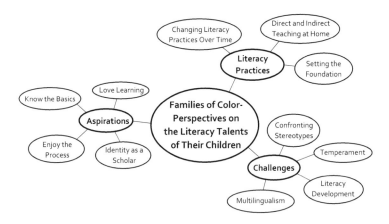

FIGURE 2.1 Families of Color – Literacy Perspectives and Experiences

discovery with more direct, adult-supported literacy teaching and learning. Our conversations also reminded me of the value of regular check-ins with families for making our literacy practices current and responsive to families' traditions and beliefs, as well as their evolving literacy talents, practices, and goals.

In this chapter, I recount current perspectives of parents whose children are in preschool, as well as retrospective views on literacy education in preschool (see the Appendix for more background on the families). Four of the parents with whom I spoke have a child currently in preschool as well as elementary school, and one parent has a current second grader whom I worked with when he was in preschool. One advantage of speaking with families of current preschoolers is that their memories of preschool literacy are fresh and immediate, while speaking with families about their children as former preschoolers provided me with a longer developmental trajectory for linking literacy learning from preschool through the primary and upper elementary grades. Both views are important as they provide different developmental windows onto how families perceive and support their children in the here-and-now of preschool literacy learning at home and school, as well as across longer periods of time and development beyond preschool.

Aspirations

In terms of family aspirations for their children's literacy learning, the families held deep-seated and passionate views on what they wanted their children to learn and achieve in terms of literacy development. The families also were clear-eyed about their views, and cognizant of the social, cultural, racial, and political ramifications of their literacy goals and aspirations.

Identity as a Scholar

Jamal and Charemon Cooks are African-American and the parents of a five-year-old son, Cameron, and ten-year-old daughter, Jamilla, both of whom attend an independent, Afro-centric P–8 school. Jamal spoke passionately and with conviction about their parental aspirations for Cameron and Jamilla, emphasizing the ultimate goal for their children to achieve a high level of academic excellence and positive identity. He and Charemon chose an Afro-centric school to instill pride, knowledge, and cultural and linguistic authenticity for their children. They value how the school emphasizes the cultural, social, and historical contributions of African-Americans in content and visuals, as well as that the majority of the teaching faculty are also African-American.

Jamal and Charemon look at education on a long-term basis, and strongly share college as a goal for both of their children and hopefully an advanced degree as well. They also believe that attaining these long-term education goals for their Cameron and Jamilla are largely based on their children's literacy levels and achievement.

> **KEY QUOTE**
>
> "We are both quite clear that literacy, learning to read and write, along with math, are *gatekeepers* to academic success and social success. We expect them to do well in school, get a job and a career, and to be self-sufficient."

An important element of their aspirations as parents concerns how early literacy learning influences their children's identities as strong and competent literacy users and creators. In preschool, for example, Jamilla loved getting the affirmation for knowing the right answers and enjoyed mastering the basics of literacy development. She also developed a love for learning and words, and Jamilla figured out how reading works by chipping away at it. Jamilla loved to spell starting in preschool, and has been very accurate since then. Jamilla's identity as a scholar has continued over the ensuing years, and she continues to interpret this identity as getting good grades, being smart, and making honor roll. Her identity as a reader still comes from reading a lot, developing an understanding of varied authors and genres, and choosing her pleasure reading at home such as series like *Diary of a Wimpy Kid*, which Jamilla constantly reads and rereads at home.

> **KEY IDEA**
>
> - Family literacy aspirations for families of Color are linked with accessing the *requisite codes of power* (Lisa Delpit) for literacy access and achievement in school
> - Family literacy aspirations are founded upon their children's evolving social, cultural, and educational competence that strengthens *personal and familial identity* (see e.g. Gloria Ladson-Billings, Geneva Gay, Mariana Souto-Manning)
> - Family literacy aspirations are passed down from one generation to the next as values and beliefs that connect families and ancestors (see e.g. Geneva Smitherman)

Challenges

In terms of the challenges that families face in supporting their children's literacy learning, families noted the challenges of supporting multilingualism, understanding and guiding children who take different developmental paths, and overcoming racial, cultural, and gender bias and stereotypes in schools.

Multilingualism and Literacy

Lidia has two children, Isaiaa and Julian, both of whom attended the preschool classroom where I worked as a part-time literacy teacher. Lidia and her husband are both of Latinx descent. The preschool classroom that Isaiaa and Julian attended has English-medium instruction as well as informal Spanish use by the head teacher, Amanda Ibarra, and at least one teaching assistant. A number of other children speak Spanish in the classroom when playing and working both inside and outside, and other teachers (such as Isaiaa and Julian's grandmother, who is a teaching assistant in another classroom at the preschool) also use Spanish informally on the playground when interacting with Spanish-speaking children.

Lidia loved the preschool's bookbag program, and she particularly noted the value of the program for encouraging her children to choose books that they liked, which encouraged them to take an interest in reading. Lidia was surprised that her current preschooler Julian chooses books in Spanish from the bookbag library. Her older child, Isaiaa, mostly chose books in English and some bilingual books. There is a section in the school library devoted to Spanish and bilingual books and teachers actively support the children's selection of these books. The children most often show an interest in these books when the teachers read a Spanish or bilingual book with the children in the classroom library, allowing children time to listen to the book and look at the pictures before children make their final choice of the book they wish to take home in their bookbag.

After noticing Julian's interest in books in Spanish, as well as Isaiaa's interest in learning more Spanish since he was aware of the several languages spoken in his second-grade classroom, Lidia realized the importance of increasing Spanish language use at home for her children. At the same time, though, she also recognized the challenge of using more Spanish at home both for herself and for her husband. Lidia and her husband had previously used Spanish at home when they didn't want their children to understand, but Lidia has since switched her goals and is intentionally using Spanish to support Julian and Isaiaa's Spanish language interests. Lidia and her husband are slowly trying to speak more Spanish at home whenever they can; it remains a challenge as they are not used to speaking Spanish as part of their daily family discourse at home, and Julian and Isaiaa are not understanding everything that is said to them. Lidia and her husband, though, remain committed to increasing their Spanish use at home and supporting their children's interests in daily conversation and books in Spanish.

Different Paths – Development and Temperament

Jamal noted that their younger child, five-year-old Cameron, has taken a different path in his early literacy learning than his older sister. When he was younger, words and books frustrated Cameron and he would get upset. The parents tried to read with Cameron every night, as they had done with Jamilla, but it was a frustrating experience for Cameron and his parents. Jamal remembers that Cameron was adamant that he could read and would take the books from his parents so they wouldn't read to him. Cameron is tall and strong for his age, and loves physical and active play; sedentary reading and working with words were very challenging for him. Jamal notes that "Cameron had to find ways to deal with this and to become comfortable in his own skin." As he turned four and then five years of age, though, Cameron became more interested in numbers as he wanted to know the correct TV channel to watch superhero cartoons. He recently started enjoying reading when Jamal bought Cameron several small Batman books, and Jamal and Cameron now read to each other four to five times a week because Cameron is interested in the material. Jamal has also fallen in love with his kindergarten teacher, and now wants to read and do well academically and socially for her. His thirst for literacy has increased, and he is asking how to spell and read words. Cameron also tries to write words more often at home and at school. He is also becoming more eager to finish his homework at home and is pleased when he's finished.

Boxed In – Confronting Stereotypes

I also spoke with Haneefah Shuaibe-Peters, who is African-American and the parent with her husband of two boys, nine-year-old Ismail and three-year-old Jacob. Ismail attends a public school and Jacob an independent preschool. Haneefah is concerned that her African-American boys are "forced into a box," forced to conform to expectations about how they should act and think in school because they are African-American boys. Haneefah sees that her children, and by extension she and her husband, confront a dominant European way of acting and thinking that doesn't always apply to Ismail and Jacob's ways of thinking, talking, and interacting, as well as their literacy interests, talents, and abilities. As Haneefah put it, "My children's schools send my children the message that you must play it safe and just show us that you can do enough." But as a concerned and supportive parent who is also an early childhood educator, Haneefah is keenly aware of the power of culturally responsive education to promote transformative education for African-American children and families. Haneefah wants a more authentic and deeper vision of her children's literacy abilities and identities.

KEY QUOTE

"I am most afraid of my African-American children forced in a box and to conform to expectations. I want them to have original thoughts and to think beyond what is in front of them."

Haneefah draws on her professional knowledge to talk with her children about her aspirations for their education and literacy learning. She wants her boys to have original thoughts and to think beyond what is in front of them, and for them to see this form of critical thinking and initiative-taking as positive and as part of their educational toolkit and identities as highly capable, hard-working African-American boys. Haneefah aspires for her children to go beyond the current educational system that only teaches children "what is there and not what is beyond." Haneefah takes direct action with her children by supporting them to find new ways to act, think, and talk in their classrooms so they can grow and achieve at the highest levels. For instance, she speaks with Ismail and encourages him to ask a lot of questions at home, hoping that this will translate to school. Haneefah recognizes that Ismail wants to meet his teacher's satisfaction, though Haneefah also understands that if Ismail asks too many questions on a topic, he might be seen as challenging in class and thus labeled a behavior problem.

While Ismail does not get into "trouble" in class due to "misbehavior," there are some African-African boys who fall into this category in his classroom, and Haneefah is deeply aware that Ismail faces a "double mirror." In this predicament, the teacher says that Ismail is doing fine in school because he's well-behaved, though this does not fully help Ismail learn and grow because the teacher may miss out on his full repertoire of language and literacy talents. As Haneefah views the double mirror, if Ismail becomes more "invisible," then his intentions, thinking, and actions may become more focused on just behaving well versus asking challenging intellectual questions, pushing his learning agenda, and developing his school identity as an inquiring and high-achieving literacy learner.

LITERACY CHALLENGES – THEORETICAL LINKS

- Children take *varied developmental paths* in their literacy learning and so need individualized, differentiated family, school, and teacher support (see e.g. the work of Anne Haas Dyson, Vivian Paley, and others)
- *Dominant discourse and participation patterns* around literacy in classrooms may not support access and equity for children of Color (see e.g. the work of Courtney Cazden and others)
- As educators and as human beings, we are *susceptible to bias and stereotypes* and lack of self-awareness for overcoming bias (see e.g. the work of Louise Derman-Sparks, John Nimmo, and others)

Practices

The families with whom I spoke are devoted and effective teachers, supporting literacy practices both from the school and those originating from or modified in home and community settings. The families are primarily interested in using and strengthening literacy practices to promote lifelong literacy learning and school success for their children, and to integrate traditional and more current literacy goals and ways of teaching and learning.

Setting the Foundation for Literacy Learning

Shyla Crowder's son Exavier, who is African American, is currently in second grade at a charter school, and I worked with Exavier when he was in preschool. (I also present some of Exavier's literacy interests and talents in later chapters of this book.) Talking with Shyla a few years removed from Exavier's preschool years allowed Shyla to reflect on what Exavier learned in preschool and the value of the literacy program for Exavier's literacy development in the primary grade years. As a second grader, Shyla said that Exavier "loves, loves, loves" reading and is reading at a third-grade level.

Shyla described how "preschool set the foundation" for Exavier's literacy development by helping him to identify the letter names and their sounds, which helped Exavier transition to kindergarten reading and learn to decode words. Exavier still likes to ask questions to clarify what he is reading and he prefers to read to Shyla, who read a lot to Exavier when he was in preschool. Shyla's sister introduced her to reading small books with Exavier when he was in preschool, and he also liked to listen to Baby Mozart music and look at the pictures.

Shyla also noted how the preschool's home-school bookbag program supported Exavier's interest in books. She remembers his love of *Froggy Goes to School* and how Exavier loved to sing "bubble bubble" every time he'd get to that part, and then he'd do a little dance. Shyla has kept the *Froggy* book that Exavier received, donated as a RIF (Reading is Fundamental) book by the local Kiwanis Club. The preschool literacy curriculum and the bookbag program inspired Exavier to enjoy reading and successfully transition to kindergarten reading.

KEY IDEA

> Driving to school each morning, Exavier reads out loud to Shyla, and usually reads a chapter book such as *Diary of a Wimpy Kid*, *Big Nate*, *In the Zone*, or *Spider-Man*.

Now in second grade, when Exavier reads and does his homework at home, he likes to listen to hip hop and R&B that Shyla plays on Pandora. It helps him focus and he does all of his reading on his own. Driving to school each morning, Exavier reads out loud to Shyla, and usually reads a chapter book such as *Diary of a Wimpy Kid*, *Big Nate*, *In the Zone*, or *Spider-Man*. Exavier's school wants him to read for at least 30 minutes each day and Shyla noted that the "books they were giving him he'd zip right through," and so they are going to the public library every Saturday to get more chapter books. Exavier reads each book until he's finished and then they return it for another book. Shyla noted that Exavier wants to return to his preschool classroom to read to the children. He can now "break down the biggest word," and if he doesn't know a word, Shyla and Exavier talk about the structure. He loves reading books and is inspired by words, and often asks about the meaning of words.

Non-Traditional Literacy Practices at Home

Maria Carriedo is the principal of the early childhood program which Isaiaa, Julian, and Exavier attended. Maria and her husband, Tony Sr., are also the parent of a current kindergartner, Tony Jr., with whom I also worked in Amanda Ibarra's classroom, and they also have twins who currently attend a local Head Start pre-school. As the principal of the early childhood program, Maria is in charge of implementing the full range of literacy goals, practices, and assessments not only for the district's program but also for the Head Start children who also attend some district preschool classrooms. As a principal and as a parent, Maria is in an unusual position – she is highly knowledgeable about high-quality early literacy practices at home and school, and is also somewhat constrained from altering much of the preschools' mandated curriculum and assessments.

Maria remembers reading and rereading books as a child, and she has tried to instill that love of reading and that practice at home with Tony when he was in preschool and also now in kindergarten. Since her three children's preschools used Spanish on an informal basis rather than as the medium of instruction, Maria mostly reads books in Spanish at home. Tony, her son, also has his own collection of Spanish and English books that he loves that include the *Pete the Cat* series and *Star Wars*, and the twins have a box of simple board books in Spanish. Maria notes that "we're trying to find more active ways for Tony to learn to read and enjoy it such as following along with *Pete the Cat* books on YouTube on our iPad. It's a bit more active for Tony." When Tony was in preschool, he loved to be active in the classroom and sitting for reading, dictation, and drawing activities was challenging for him. Although Maria runs a program that focuses on providing a high-quality literacy foundation for preschoolers of Color, as a parent she also wonders if Tony, as an active child who loves to move and build things, would have rebelled at doing more literacy-related tasks. Now in kindergarten, Tony is just now doing math facts and talking about his stories, and he now thinks he can read. Maria also questions if he'd be reading if she and her husband had read to Tony every day when he was younger.

Having experienced preschool literacy as a parent with Tony, Maria has new aspirations and employs new teaching practices for the twins. Maria now realizes that she and her husband want to be held more accountable for their children's preschool literacy learning. For instance, in the home-school bookbag program, Maria favors families writing down the names of each book that they read with their children, and to read more books and even do a little structured homework. Maria wants all of her children's teachers to know that they are reading at home, and to know what she and her husband are reading to their children.

Homework is also a dilemma for Maria as a parent as an ECE leader. She hears many Latinx and African-American parents say that they want homework at home, but the research says that's not appropriate for preschool. As a Latinx parent, the homework piece is important for Maria, "It symbolizes that as a parent I am doing my part for myself, my family, and for the school." Maria recognizes that many Latinx and African-American parents were "themselves raised old school," and that she and her husband need to employ more non-traditional literacy practices with their children such as collaborative storytelling in the car, reading signs, and asking open-ended questions, why-questions, and prompts to expand their languages and literacies.

KEY QUOTE

"As a Latinx parent, the homework piece is important for me – it *symbolizes* that as a parent I am doing my part for myself, my family, and for the school."

Now that Tony is in kindergarten and is doing some homework, this has given Maria's husband, Tony Sr., a new important role at home. He loves helping his son with homework, and as working parents who get home at 7:00 p.m., they now have down time from 7:00 p.m. to 8:00 p.m., and Tony Sr. sits with young Tony and they do the homework together. They do projects, dictation, and literacy-related worksheets. Tony Sr. helps Tony when he gets frustrated, and plays a strong supportive and scaffolding role in their homework sessions. Their bond has deepened as father and son, and this has had a positive, motivating effect on young Tony, who recently wanted to read an entire book with his father.

For Lidia and her husband, parents of preschooler Julian and second-grader Isaiaa, they have also worked to complement and extend their children's literacy learning in school. Just as Maria's husband, Tony Sr., takes Tony Jr. to the library on a regular basis, Lidia's husband also has a regular library routine with Julian. While Lydia is at work at the hospital, Julian and his father visit the local library every two weeks to check out new books; Julian chooses his own books, and his father makes some suggestions when Julian doesn't know which books he wants.

Direct and Indirect Literacy Teaching at Home

When Jamilla was in preschool, Jamal and Charemon read books to her five nights a week and Jamilla had a bookshelf of full of books at age three. When they noticed Jamilla's deep interest in books and reading, they switched from Jamilla's home daycare setting to a more formal preschool setting. While the daycare provided a lot of love, Christian songs, and learning how to treat each other well, they recognized the need for Jamilla to have more of an academic challenge. The culture of the school, with students working a grade ahead, has been an excellent academic fit for Jamilla. Jamal recognized that from an early age Jamilla wanted and needed to work hard to excel in language and literacy.

At home, Jamal and Charemon created a literacy-rich environment, read with and to Jamilla at night, and they never used baby talk with her. When she was a toddler, Jamal and Charemon were intent on modeling literacy achievement for Jamilla, modeling how to put together sentences, syntax, and language tone. When Jamilla was two years old, they used flashcards with her that had pictures on one side and the corresponding words on the other. Jamal recalled that both his mother and Charemon's mother stayed home with them when they were young, and used similar teaching practices, using flash cards, then moving on to sight words and then reading.

In preschool, Jamilla was reading by age four and thrived on writing daily sight words and then sentences with conventional spelling, all through direct instruction. Jamal and Charemon liked this instruction because it was getting results for Jamilla, and they decided to do more creative and open-ended forms of writing, scribbling, and art at home to complement the more direct instruction at school. As Jamilla's reading skills deepened and expanded, she read more and more at school and at home, and Jamal and Charemon have kept pace with this advancement at home. Currently, as Jamilla attends fifth grade, Jamal and Charemon have a new system for reading at home that is both open-ended and direct instruction. They have created a shared hand-off system for reading books with Jamilla. While one parent reads a book with Jamilla (which that parent has read earlier), the other parent reads a second book in preparation for reading the next book with Jamilla once the first parent is done. This way, both parents keep pace with Jamilla's reading and guide her deep understanding of books, such as making connections amongst characters and understanding the characters' motivations. This process has also helped Jamal and Charemon to recognize their respective literacy strengths as parents – Jamal likes to apply the books to Jamilla's current experiences and Charemon enjoys working on character analysis with Jamilla.

KEY QUOTE

"We tried to expose Cameron to literacy and hoped he'd come to it when he was ready."

For supporting Cameron's reading, they have taken a different approach. As a high-energy child, Jamal and Charemon tried to read to Cameron at night when he was younger but it was challenging. As Jamal put it, "We tried to expose Cameron to literacy and hoped he'd come to it when he was ready." Cameron also had a bookshelf at home full of books, and a literacy-rich environment, and Cameron would grab books and try to read but he was not interested in the doing the work to read. Now that he is older and in kindergarten, he has become more interested in reading and asks how to spell words. Jamal reads four to five books with him each night, and Cameron loves *Batman* books, which he "reads" and then gives to Jamal to read. This process was Cameron's idea.

There are 20 sight words listed at the front of the *Batman* books, and Jamal reads several words out loud as Cameron points to the words, and then Cameron points to several other words as Jamal reads these words out loud. Jamal loves this collaborative effort, and supports whatever is going to get Cameron to read. He and Charemon are now reading one book at night to Cameron from his box of ten books in his room. Occasionally, Cameron will look at the other books on his own, and his parents help Cameron with his kindergarten homework, such as tracing a sentence and then copying it, which he enjoys more than reading as it is more active.

Lidia and her husband also do a lot of reading and writing with their children, Isaiaa and Julian, at home. Julian and Isaiaa like to work together, and Julian learns from his older brother and Isaiaa enjoys the opportunity to teach and support his younger brother. This cross-age support and teaching rarely happens in preschools, as preschool children are often separated from primary-age children. Julian and Isaiaa read books together at home, though sometimes Julian likes to read and sometimes he doesn't. At home, Isaiaa has to read at least 20 minutes a day, and sometimes he reads Dr. Seuss and other books from his second-grade classroom to Julian at home. They sit next to each other so Julian can listen to the story and look at the pictures, and Julian mostly listens to his brother read and enjoys it. Lidia and her husband also read to Julian and sometimes to Isaiaa.

Lidia noted that Julian likes to read more at school, which I can also attest to, as he loves read-alouds with me in his preschool classroom and is an active and engaged conversant about the books. At home, Julian is most interested in books with facts about sports or cars or animals. Lidia believes that knowledge is power and encourages both of her children to read. At home, Julian likes to ask questions about what is going on in the stories and to point out small details in the book's pictures. Julian will sometimes ask questions that are a bit mature for his age, or will make an observation that will surprise Lidia. For instance, there might be a page with visuals and if Julian feels that Lidia is not paying enough attention to the book, Julian will point out a detail in the visuals such as a character's facial expression to keep Lidia engaged. In other instances when Isaiaa is reading his book and asks his parents a question, Julian will listen in on the conversation and ask his own questions modeled on Isaiaa's questions.

Changing Literacy Practices Over Time

Haneefah has implemented a range of literacy practices at home for Ismail and Jacob. When Ismail was an infant, Haneefah read many stories to him, and during his toddler and preschool years, Haneefah continued to read and also support Ismail's drawing. By trying different activities at home, Haneefah learned that there is a relationship and balance between reading, drawing, and writing – "You can't focus on one and expect to get both. Reading and writing have to be focused on to get a balance."

KEY QUOTE

"You can't focus just on one and expect to get both. Reading and writing have to be focused on to get a balance."

With Jacob, her younger son, Haneefah also looks for new ways to promote language learning and to build on Jacob's musical talents. Jacob loves to listen to a song and catch onto the rhythm, the beat, and his auditory talents are strong. He can also have a real conversation on many topics, and Haneefah is focused on promoting back-and-forth conversations with Jacob. She also supports Jacob's interest in language and meaning-making by making sure she understands what he says. For instance when Jacob says, "Mom that was a really good question, wasn't it?" Haneefah extends his interest with supportive reasons. Haneefah also consciously uses sarcasm and jokes to help Jacob understand their purpose and how to use language in context to maintain the meaning of words.

Haneefah recognized that as a toddler, Jacob had different interests and talents than Ismail, who was more interested in reading from an early age. With Jacob she decided to focus on visuals, and tried a picture process of taking photos of Jacob's activities in the house, diapering, basketball, playing with toys, and she collected these in a binder starting when Jacob was 16 months old. Haneefah and Jacob looked at the pictures together, and Haneefah added narration to their picture browsing. Now as a three-and-a-half-year-old, Jacob regularly goes to the binder and tells Haneefah a whole story about himself, using words like "larger," "smaller," and "spiky," descriptive words rooted in his funds of knowledge. Jacob has also integrated new vocabulary and syntax. For instance, he now notices that he wore "black shoes with Velcro" whereas as a toddler he only noted the "black shoes." Jacob also compares and contrasts his experiences over time such as when he observed, "I don't wear diapers now."

Chapter Summary and Reflections

The families profiled in this chapter spoke eloquently and with passion about their literacy aspirations, challenges, and practices for understanding and supporting their children's literacy learning in and out of school. Their perspectives indicate the families' deep caring for their children's literacy development, their awareness of the long-term nature of literacy learning, their vision of their children as lifelong literacy learners, the small and large challenges that they and their children face in literacy learning both in the home and in preschools, and the intentionality and strength behind the families' literacy practices to support their children's strengths, interests, and needs.

In terms of *aspirations*, the families articulated deeply rooted hopes and dreams for their children that drew upon their own childhoods and their vision for their children's social, cultural, literate, and educational success. For instance, Jamal's emphasis on his children's identities as scholars struck a deep chord with me. Like the other families that I spoke with, Jamal and Charemon want their children to aspire to their greatest heights in their literacy interest, engagement, and learning, and for this literacy journey to be integrated with their evolving identities as strong, competent learners acquiring the foundation for successful lifelong learning.

In terms of *challenges*, the families described certain obstacles that we as educators must attend to in both in our teaching psyches and in our teaching practices as we conceptualize and enact strength-based literacy teaching. For example, Haneefah expressed her concern that her two African-American children might be forced into a box in their classrooms and schools, forced to conform to certain pre-conceptions that educators and schools might have about the literacy, learning, and behavioral needs of African-American boys. Haneefah wants, though, for her children to have original thoughts and to think beyond what is in front of them, not to conform to a European model of behavior and thinking, and play it safe and show their teachers that they just do enough. She wants more for her children; they deserve more.

In terms of *practices*, Shyla supports her son Exavier's literacy in school by continuing to read with him at home, a practice that they started with interest and success when Exavier was in preschool and enjoyed the home-school bookbag program. Shyla takes Exavier every Saturday to the public library to return his book and to check out a new one. This consistent routine shows Exavier the value of literacy out of school, and of supporting reading in school, and it provides Shyla and Exavier a collaborative and supportive familial foundation for his literacy learning. When this kind of bonding experience is extended in other ways, as happens daily as Exavier reads out loud to Shyla during their morning commute to school, Shyla and Exavier deepen their familial relationship and bonds.

On a personal and professional note, I myself was surprised at times by the families' literacy perspectives, challenges, and practices that I was unaware of, and that provided me with a larger canvas in which to view their children's literacy talents and knowledge. I realized, too, that even with my length of time in the early childhood field, and years of experience teaching early literacy, I still need (and always will) to stay current on family perspectives and experiences regarding the literacy talents and interests of children of Color. I hope that you as readers also experienced an awakening in your thoughts and views on the talents and strengths of families of Color in terms of literacy education, and that as we go forward in this book we can carry along the focus on the aspirations, challenges, and practices of families of Color.

I also point out here, in this closing section of this chapter, a number of theoretical links to Chapter 1 that arose in reflecting on the families' literacy perspectives and practices.

FAMILY LITERACY PERSPECTIVES AND PRACTICES – THEORETICAL LINKS

- *"Ways with words"* (Shirley Brice Heath and interpreters)
- A *liberatory education* (Paulo Freire and interpreters)
- *"Funds of knowledge"* (Luis Moll and interpreters)
- *"Generative spaces"* and *"asset pedagogies"* (H. Samy Alim, Django Paris, and others)
- *Race reflection, revoicing, and reflexivity* (H. Richard Milner and others)

We can see how the socio-cultural frame of *ways with words* first articulated by Shirley Brice Heath can be intimately played out in discourse and literacy practices between home and school. For instance, Lidia, the parent of Julian and Isaiaa, noticed her children's increased interest in the Spanish language and in reading and listening to books in Spanish. She and her husband then began a shift in the multilingual discourse patterns in their home to honor and support their children's increasing interest in multilingualism and cultural connections.

We can see elements of *liberatory education, generative spaces, and asset pedagogies* in several of the practices that the families have instituted to support their children's literacy growth. For instance, Maria and her husband, parents of preschool-age twins and a kindergartner, realized that they "themselves were raised old school" and that they must now acquire more transformative literacy practices such as collaborative storytelling in the car, reading signs, and asking open-ended questions, why-questions, and prompts to expand their children's Spanish and English.

The families also rely on their personal, familial, and *cultural funds of knowledge* for supporting their children's literacy interests, experiences, and talents. For instance, Haneefah and her son Jacob enjoy looking at pictures in books together, and now that Jacob is in preschool, Haneefah has added a layer of narration to their shared picture browsing. Jacob regularly goes to the binder of pictures that they have created together and tells Haneefah a whole story about himself, using words like "larger," "smaller," and "spiky," words rooted in his daily lived experiences at home.

Finally, certain families engage in a process of race reflection, revoicing, and reflexivity to both counter and support their children's school-based literacy learning. For instance, Jamal and Charemon are keenly aware of the challenge and need to support their children's identities as African-American children and learners. They have selected an Afro-centric school for their children's early childhood and elementary school education because of the presence of African-American teachers and the school's emphasis on African-American history, values, and traditions. Jamal and Charemon also hold a deep belief in their children as educational scholars who are acquiring the social, cultural, and educational capital to become highly competent lifelong literacy learners. Their view of literacy achievement also takes in the value of literacy for future economic self-sufficiency and personal well-being.

As we move into the next chapter on educators' perspectives on the literacy talents and knowledge of children of Color, please keep in mind the aspirations, challenges, and practices of the families in this chapter. The families' experiences and viewpoints are a critical foundation for us as educators to reflect on our understanding of the literacy talents and abilities of children of Color, and to deepen the process of changing and strengthening our literacy goals, curriculum, and practices. Before turning to the next chapter, consider the end-of-chapter reflections in the call-out box as a way to prompt your thinking.

END-OF -CHAPTER REFLECTIONS

- Which *literacy aspirations* from the families presented in this chapter resonated most deeply with you? How might you incorporate some of these aspirations into your literacy goals, environment, material, instructional strategies, assessments, and partnership with families?
- Which *literacy challenges* from the families did you find most intriguing and valuable? Have you experienced similar challenges from the families you have or currently work with?
- Which *literacy practices* from the families did you find most appealing and of interest? How might you work to support families' literacy strategies at home and in the community, and how might some of these strategies make their way into your preschool setting? Conversely, are

there some classroom literacy practices that can be adapted by families in children's homes and communities?

- What new ideas has this chapter sparked that you might pursue to strengthen your *dialogue and collaboration* around literacy with your families?
- What new *teaching practices* are you now interested in pursuing after reading about the families' literacy beliefs, goals, and practices?

3

EDUCATOR PERSPECTIVES ON LITERACY EDUCATION – MELDING PHILOSOPHIES AND PRACTICES

OPENING REFLECTIONS

- What views and perspectives do you hold most dear regarding successful literacy education for young children?
- What are your greatest hopes and dreams for the social and literacy achievement of young children of Color?
- Which aspects of your teaching beliefs, philosophies, and practices would you most like to strengthen to improve your literacy teaching for young children of Color?
- What specific next steps would you like to take in this process of deepening your philosophy of literacy education and teaching practices to support children of Color?

In this chapter, I discuss the perspectives and experiences of several educators regarding how they conceptualize and implement a strength-based approach to the literacy education of preschool children of Color. In reflecting on my conversations and my knowledge of these educators, some of whom I have known and worked with for over 20 years, I have organized the material in this chapter into the following five main sections – foundational philosophies of schooling and learning, the literacy talents of children of Color, high-quality literacy instruction, adapting curriculum to fit children's literacy needs, and professional inquiry and educational change. These sections work together to create an important backdrop of teacher philosophies and approaches for the upcoming chapters focusing on specific areas of children's literacy education and learning.

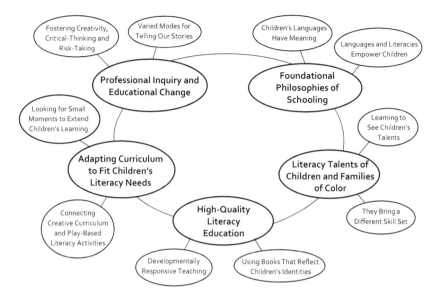

FIGURE 3.1   Educators' Perspectives on Strength-Based Literacy Education—Key Elements

Foundational Philosophies of Schooling and Learning

Formulating a philosophy of education often gets short-shrift in preservice and inservice early childhood professional development, as we spend more time on child development, curriculum, instruction, and assessment. Yet formulating (and tweaking as we go) a philosophy of education rooted in who we are as individuals, cultural beings, and educators helps support strength-based literacy education for children of Color (Figure 3.1).

Languages and Literacies Empower Children

Carlos Castillejo, who has taught preschool and the primary grades in English and Spanish, strongly believes in personal, professional, and political connections that form his philosophy of language and literacy education and work with children of Color and their families. Born and raised in Mexico, Carlos is keenly aware of the power of language and literacy to empower young children both in and out of school, and also how contemporary schooling can limit children's language and literacy identities and sense of power as learners. His literacy teaching is driven by his passion and a philosophy of education that promotes young children as own-ing their languages, literacies, and schooling careers.

> Who owns language? Give the language to the children, and if you give them the power and the words, then you give them the power to speak. But

if you are saying that they are not learning English, or speaking or reading or understanding, then you institutionalize the power of learning and the children are not getting the language they need. If the school always controls the languages and literacies that are taught, then who owns the language? Who owns the power? If we change the structure of teaching, then we change the relations of power, and then we can see children as learners and the institution of schooling can acknowledge their talents.

KEY QUOTE

If the school always controls the languages and literacies that are taught, then who owns the language? Who owns the power?

Carlos also strongly believes in literacy curriculum as founded upon a vision of education that not only expects results but also respects the process of learning. In his five years of teaching in U.S. public schools, he has only taught from a teaching manual and not from a rich and deep curriculum accompanied by professional development that guides teachers in an agentic and transformative curricular process. Carlos believes that teaching from a manual has prevented him from developing high-quality literacy instruction, though it has taught Carlos the powerful insight that "if we don't know the curriculum, then we don't know how it can impact the education of the children we are serving."

Carlos believes that a rich and high-quality literacy curriculum is founded upon children's multiple intelligences rather than their deficits and what they lack. He places two important questions at the foundation of his teaching philosophy around children's knowledge and meaning-making – "Why limit our understanding of reality in one single direction? How can I address as many of children's intelligences as I can?" Keeping these questions in mind reminds Carlos to teach to children's intelligences even if it makes us uncomfortable as we focus on children's needs rather than on our teaching strengths.

Children's Languages Have Meaning

Dawn Douangsawang, a Lao/English bilingual preschool teacher, has eight years of preschool teaching experience first at a Montessori school and then at an academic-focused school. Dawn was born and raised in the San Francisco Bay area, and was not allowed to use English at home growing up as her parents highly prized maintaining their Laotian culture and language. She remembers many oral stories in Laotian growing up, and her parents' insistence on not losing their culture. But when she entered kindergarten at a public school, Dawn had a friend with whom she spoke Laotian in the classroom. Their kindergarten teacher discouraged their speaking Laotian, and Dawn got in trouble a lot in the classroom. She went into her shell and became quiet. Dawn wanted to raise her hand, but she didn't, fearing that the teachers and children would laugh at her for not knowing a certain English word. Her teachers did not ask her what she was doing in class, or what she understood and was learning.

These early childhood experiences and memories have remained with Dawn, and they form the basis and the motivation for her teaching philosophy and her view on the literacy education of young children of Color. Denied her language as a source of strength as a child in school, as a teacher Dawn strongly believes in letting her students talk in their own languages – "Deep down, I know their language has meaning, and the children might need our support and clarification."

KEY QUOTE

"Deep down, I know their language has meaning, and the children might need our support and clarification."

Dawn also believes in the value of personal and social connections with children as individuals, and values spending one-on-one time with children, finding out their interests, telling stories with each child for enjoyment and fun, and asking open-ended questions that draw out children's individual personalities and talents. Remembering her early school experiences of not talking and not understanding in preschool, Dawn values supporting multilingual learners by rephrasing her language and adjusting her speech, especially when children give a blank face and appear not to understand. Her current school emphasizes the learning of Spanish and Japanese, two languages that Dawn does not know but is determined to learn, and she also asks children how they say a concept or object in their own language so they don't feel socially and culturally isolated as she did as a young child.

A Strength-Based Image of the Child

Isauro Michael Escamilla, who was born and raised in Mexico, has taught for at least two decades as a Spanish/English dual language teacher in the San Francisco Unified School District. His upbringing in Mexico is an important component of his identity as a teacher and as an adult learner. His schooling was very traditional with many worksheets, but his mother loved to tell him stories of her own rural childhood and traditional stories and folktales, which helped Isauro imagine a world that he did not live in but which his mother had. Moving from Mexico to the U.S. as a young adult, attending school became a constant in his learning and growth as an educator. He strongly believes in the value of continual professional growth and community service, to maintain the feeling of learning something new and to believe that education will move him forward and succeed. His parents instilled in Isauro a deep belief that you are more likely to do well and be independent in life with an education and willingness to volunteer for a good cause. Isauro carries these beliefs and values into his teaching, working with children and families of mostly Latinx descent to ensure that they receive the skills, knowledge, and reassurance that they need to succeed.

KEY QUOTE

"If I believe that all children are bright and resourceful and talented, I need to highlight that for myself, my children and my families."

As a teacher who knows the educational and social values and beliefs on both sides of the Mexico/US border, he is also keenly aware of the need to use positive images to portray the social, educational, and literary lives of young children of Color.

> It is now more important than ever for me to portray children of Color in a very positive light. When we hear on the news that Latino men are bad people, that's an impact on all of us, when we hear that kind of language, it makes me feel that I am the opposite, I am good. It is my job to highlight the good qualities that the children have. If I believe that all children are bright and resourceful and talented, I need to highlight that for myself, my children and my families. A lot of the image of the child is closely related to the image of the teacher; it has to be a parallel path or vision. The self-image of the teacher is tied up with the image of children.

For Isauro, everything that children of Color do, what they say, the artifacts that they build, are all an expression of what they know, their knowledge and understanding, and how they perceive the world. This fits with Isauro's passion for the Project Approach and the ideas and philosophies of Reggio Emilia educators, which he and his colleagues integrate to create a positive image of children of Color as competent, resourceful, and creative learners and literacy creators.

Literacy Talents of Children and Families of Color

Envisioning and implementing strength-based literacy education is based upon foundational philosophies of learning and school as well learning to recognize and appreciate the literacy talents of children of Color.

Learning to See Their Talents

Gaya Kakulawela has taught preschool for five years in San Francisco. Growing up in Colombo, Sri Lanka, Gaya was taught in Sinhala and English. As a child traveling from Colombo to the middle of the country to visit her grandparents on the bus, Gaya remembers that the family read billboards and store signs in both languages. Literacy was socially interactive and often turned into games like I Spy on the bus. It was a slow bus, and they read the signs along the three-hour bus journey that only took 45 minutes by car.

Growing up with the experience of literacy as social and communal, Gaya has looked for these connections with the children of Color with whom she has taught. As an undergraduate in the U.S., Gaya taught four years for the Jumpstart program that places undergraduates in preschool classrooms to support children's literary development. Gaya found it valuable to read the same book multiple times with the children, to read for enjoyment, and also to promote vocabulary and comprehension. This was her initial preservice foundation for learning to recognize and understand how to observe and teach to children's strengths.

After graduation, Gaya taught at the same school for two years as a teacher and then three more years as a head teacher. The English-medium school serves approximately 160 mostly Latinx children born in the U.S. to first-generation families. Gaya's perception of the children's talents has deepened and broadened over her first five years of teaching. In her first year of teaching, Gaya communicated with those children who spoke English, and while she was aware of the other children who spoke Spanish, her Spanish-speaking colleagues were the ones who mostly taught and worked with the Spanish-speaking children. Subsequently, Gaya learned some Spanish from the bingo game the children loved, and when she started to say some words in Spanish the children began to flock to her. Gaya asked them simple questions about the words and they all celebrated when someone won a bingo game. Their bingo time involved a mix of social and academic learning, and recognizing letters and sounding out sounds and phonemic awareness in English and some Spanish. Gaya tried to have conversations with the primarily Spanish-speaking children during the bingo games, even if it was minimal. From this early teaching experience, Gaya believes that even if she does not speak children's languages, it's so important to make an effort to learn some of their language and to connect with children to support their literacy.

Gaya has also learned to guide children's literacy learning as based on children's interests and experiences. For instance, she tries to find ways to link a story to children's lives and their family structures, if they were adopted or their families had to emigrate – "I've learned that the children and I can build literacy on anything. I can build literacy around who they are and who their families are, and I connect stories and words to the personal and the social." In her current role as the head teacher, Gaya is also eager to create more pedagogical space for linking children's multilingual talents and their literacy learning by working with her colleagues. Gaya has one bilingual colleague, and Gaya is eager to create more Spanish language and literacy use in their classroom. For instance, the teachers read a book in Spanish once a week, and Gaya wants the classroom to read two Spanish books each week in the morning, and she will ask her co-teacher to speak only in Spanish.

KEY QUOTE

"I've learned that the children and I can build literacy on anything. I can build literacy around who they are and who their families are, and I connect stories and words to the personal and the social."

Gaya has also learned to recognize and support the literacy hopes and needs of the children's families. She feels that she really didn't have a strength-based view of the parents and their involvement with their children when she started teaching. Over the first five years of her teaching, upon speaking with more and families and getting to know their histories and stories, Gaya has strengthened her awareness of how parents of Color are involved with their children's education. Although they may not necessarily attend all school events, Gaya now knows that they want their children to learn their numbers and their letters and will support their children to practice at home. Gaya has learned that many parents want more direct instruction and guidance, asking Gaya how they can get more of the materials that she uses in the classroom and ideas for helping their children's literacy learning at home. In addition to talking with parents about literacy support at home, Gaya is looking for new ways to support parents' understanding of young children's literacy development, and is searching for short articles in Spanish that they might find useful. Gaya also believes that it is also important for some of her teaching colleagues to have access to articles in Spanish on literacy teaching.

A Different Skill Set

Maria Sujo is a veteran Spanish/English bilingual college instructor and administrator, who currently serves as the Kindergarten Readiness Manager for the Oakland Unified School District. Maria's work with children and families of Color over the years has taught her the value of making their educational and literacy talents, interests, and needs visible and known. From her work with mostly immigrant children whose families speak a number of different languages, some of which do not have literacy equivalents, Maria now strongly believes in recognizing the children's and families' educational strengths. She argues that while many talents of children of Color are not as readily apparent as children from the dominant U.S. culture, they have special talents to draw pictures, represent objects and ideas, create things, and are interested in stories, music, and movement.

They are learning English and scan the environment and read social cues from other children and teachers to know what is coming next. Some of the children and families in her district are speakers of Mam (a Mayan language) that has no written language equivalent and so the parents are not "literate" in the traditional sense. Interacting with print, then, in schools is a new concept for the Mam-speaking children, but when the children scribble pictures it shows their interest in wanting to communicate and express themselves, and they then need help from their teachers to connect their drawings with dictation in English.

Maria believes that the foundational challenge for teachers and administrators is to become aware of and understand how to support children and families who don't know how to interact with print, and have a different relationship to literacy and the social cues around literacy learning at school. Although Maria recognizes that the children with whom she works have some catching up to do in terms of literacy learning, "the children bring a lot of social and linguistic talent to this effort, and different qualities than families who own lots of books and go on trips to the library. The children that I work worth bring a different skill set."

KEY QUOTE

"The children bring a lot of social and linguistic talent to this effort, and different qualities than families who own lots of books and go on trips to the library. The children bring a different skill set."

Maria's strong conviction to make visible the language and literacy talents of children of Color is based in large part on her awareness and support of the families' strengths and needs. She views families as an integral part of children's learning, and invites them to play an important role in their children's schooling. In making these early social, literacy, and institutional connections in preschool, Maria and her colleagues can learn what families bring to the school in terms of literacy talents and funds of knowledge. In her current family engagement role, Maria finds out if there are books in the children's homes, and how to support the children and families where they are in their literacy learning.

I don't assume that everyone knows how to read, or that they are scoring low on a literacy test because they are not smart. For example, I was recently translating in a parent conference and the parents' child was not recognizing letters in transitional kindergarten and her parents had opposite schedules at home to help the child, and every day a different immigration appointment. So learning to navigate U.S. schools and other institutions takes a lot of time and effort, and so I try to connect with families to know where they are coming from, to be allowed access to their worlds and to learn what is happening with their children. After three years in my current position, the more I am in schools and the neighborhoods of refugees and newcomers, their learning needs become more apparent and I see how globalization and immigration affect children's learning, everything from learning how to identify letters to interacting with print.

Maria's work has allowed her to make the learning and literacy talents of children and families of Color more visible and to place them at the center of literacy learning at home and school.

High-Quality Literacy Education

Our foundational philosophies of teaching and literacy education and our perspectives on the literacy talents of young children of Color directly influence high-quality literacy education. This effective approach is based less on a revolving door of "best practices" and more on how and why teachers and educators utilize and adapt our foundational philosophies and recognition of children's talents to create high-access, high-quality literacy instruction.

Developmentally Responsive Teaching

Amanda Ibarra, the head teacher in the mixed-age classroom in which I taught, is a Spanish/English educator who has taught for 15 years. She has consistently worked with children of Color in public school settings, and strongly believes in looking for ways to strengthen children's literacy talents through a developmentally responsive literacy curriculum. Amanda's vision of developmentally responsive teaching integrates a strong belief in the value of play along with consistent attention to children's intellectual development and literacy learning, which in turn is influenced by the program's mandated assessments and kindergarten readiness expectations.

As a teacher of Color who learned English in kindergarten herself, and who often knew the answers to teachers' questions but was too shy to speak, Amanda creates a classroom environment responsive to children's developmental language and literacy needs and talents. She strongly believes that "children's voices need to be heard, and once you create that supportive and responsive environment, the children speak up even more." To support children's voices both socially and in terms of children's literacy education, Amanda places a high priority on oral language, word knowledge, stories, and songs in English and Spanish, which are the hallmarks of developmentally and culturally responsive literacy teaching.

> **KEY QUOTE**
>
> "Children's voices need to be heard, and once you create that support-ive and responsive environment, the children speak up even more."

For instance, during whole-group book read-alouds, Amanda encourages children to be comfortable making any connections they can to a story or a book. Amanda accepts any of their questions or comments as valid responses to the story or book in a whole-group setting, and then works with children individually or in small groups, where she can fine-tune her questions and prompts about books and stories to be responsive to children's developmental interests, knowledge, and language. In this way, she adjusts the degree of difficulty of the vocabulary, structures, and content that she uses with the children. Amanda also uses drawing, painting, clay, and music to support children's connections to books and stories, which encourages children's connections without the added pressure of oral language production and comprehension.

Currently, to develop children's talents with and understanding of word meanings and words in context, Amanda is experimenting with new ways to introduce vocabulary as linked with content in developmentally responsive ways. For instance, when the children were interested in winter animals, Amanda supported the children's learning through books, stories, conversation, dictation, and art. An important part of the children's learning involved Amanda's introduction of sophisticated vocabulary and terms such as "arctic," "winter animals," and "glacier" and important concepts such as what happens to water at different temperature levels. As the content of the activities were also new to Amanda, she challenged herself to learn along with the children, and uses the iPad to look up information, key terms, and helpful visuals along with the children. Amanda, her colleagues, and the children also created a theme box of small winter animals, and Amanda and her colleagues and the children also created information visuals about winter animals. In this way, Amanda not only models risk-taking as an adult learner but also models developmentally responsive learning processes for teachers and children to learn together at the same time.

Culturally Responsive Teaching

Prenties Brown has taught for six years at a Head Start preschool in Oakland, and places culturally responsive teaching at the heart of her teaching and literacy education. Prenties and her colleagues are all multilingual speakers, and value incorporating children's home languages into the curriculum, and often read to students in Arabic, Spanish, Amharic, and English. Prenties and her colleagues also often talk about other languages, and use the classroom walls to display and discuss words in different languages.

Prenties also recognizes that her children's knowledge of literacy comes in many forms and makes itself apparent at different levels. In her teaching role, and in her additional role as curricular mentor with her colleagues, Prenties works with her children at their individual levels. One current student is working on identifying letter names and sounds, another on writing just the first letter of his name, and another is writing simple three-letter words.

Prenties and her colleagues are culturally sensitive to the need to communicate with children's families about their children's literacy needs and talents, and to recognize the importance of building home–school literacy bridges. Prenties and her colleagues regularly communicate the children's literacy talents and needs to their families. Each month the teachers create the children's individual development plan for each developmental domain. This helps parents know where their children are in their development, what the teachers are teaching in the classrooms, and how the parents might support their children's literacy and general learning at home. Prenties has found that in general her students are learning to recognize letters and letter sounds and have print awareness because of the parents' involvement in their learning.

As an educator of Color, Prenties is always searching for high-quality multilingual, multicultural literature that speaks to the identities, interests, and traditions of her children and families. She is especially interested in selecting and using books with language and words that have a compelling impact on what children remember and retain when books are read as read-alouds. Prenties also seeks high-quality children's literature with visuals so that her children can see themselves in the illustrations and the content.

SAMPLE TITLES OF CULTURALLY RESPONSIVE CHILDREN'S LITERATURE USED BY PRENTIES WITH HER CHILDREN

- *Wings* by Christopher Myers
- *Chocolate Me* by Taye Diggs
- *I Love My Hair* by Natasha Tarpley
- *I'm a Pretty Little Black Girl* by Betty K. Bynum
- *The Sifrah Glider* by Ahmad AbdulGhani Al Redha
- *Sitti's Secrets* by Naomi Shihab Nye
- *Viva Frida* by Yuyi Morales
- *Green Is a Chile Pepper* by Roseanne Greenfield Thong
- *Growing Up with Tamales/Los Tamales de Ana* by Gwendolyn Zepeda

Deeply aware that African-American and Latinx males are incarcerated at more than five times the rate of Whites, Prenties selects books that boys of Color are drawn to that show characters who look like them and who are engaged in creative, active experiences and adventures. Prenties believes that these kinds of books encourage boys of Color to have a broad view of all the things they can do now as children and in the future as adults.

Each week, Prenties conducts three read-alouds of the same book, as well as doing story walks with objects that the children can touch and see as connected with the story. If the story is very long, Prenties breaks up the book into sections and uses creative ways to enhance the children's engagement with and learning of the text's meaning and its relation to their classroom community and out-of-school lives. Prenties also devotes longer periods of time to certain books that capture the children's attention and imagination, and connect deeply to their identities.

For example, Prenties devoted a month's work of study to Christopher Myers's *Wings*, which has a powerful message and illustrations that resonated both with Prenties and with her children. Prenties has learned that a number of her children of Color know who Trayvon Martin was, as their mothers are teaching them how to act and dress, and not to walk into certain neighborhoods by themselves. Employing foundational ideas from the frameworks of asset pedagogies and generative spaces, Prenties uses *Wings* to talk about feelings with her children, and if they see something that bothers them, tell an adult, and for children and adults to stand together and help each other. In the spirit of anti-bias education and reflective teaching, Prenties is also aware of the types of lessons that Anglo/White children are learning about children of Color from literature and other sources, and although she does not work with Anglo/White children, Prenties is deeply cognizant that what we learn in literature as children stays with us for a long time.

Adapting Curriculum to Fit Children's Needs

Mr. Jon, Alma Lyons, and Hannah Nguyen have taught preschool for 33, 37, and 16 years respectively. They work together at a large Head Start preschool of ten classrooms with children of Color from primarily immigrant families who speak a number of languages. The teachers use Creative Curriculum to teach literacy, and given their extensive experience in supporting children and families of Color, the teachers complement and adapt this published curriculum to fit the social, cultural, and literacy talents and needs of their children.

The teachers utilize hands-on and play-based projects and investigations to promote children's discovery-based literacy learning. The school has had professional development work in both the Project Approach and also the Reggio Emilia approach, as well as more recent work on learning stories from New Zealand. The teachers integrate elements of these approaches into their adaptations of their foundational Creative Curriculum teaching. Each week they have a topic for investigation, and they are currently in week four of investigation four, "Who takes care of trees?" The teachers use the curricular prompts to provoke the children's content interest and to stimulate conversation, attention to words and word meanings, books and stories, and to other literacy-related activities. Repeated readings and picture walks are especially emphasized, which help the children quickly begin to anticipate the book's language and content. In the first reading, the teachers "read" the pictures so children can understand the book via the pictures without the added cognitive and linguistic pressure of the oral language demands of syntax and vocabulary. During subsequent readings, the children learn to tell parts of the story themselves and eventually like to "read" it to another child.

In their investigation of trees, the teachers use open-ended questions to lead the children in discussions about living vs. nonliving things and use visuals such as charts to help the children understand the concepts. The teachers and children go outside to compare the trees on the yard and around the school, and the children identify the trees that change leaves and those that don't. They then compare what they see with the classroom visuals, such as a chart with pictures of trees and key academic vocabulary in English and Spanish, "evergreen" and "deciduous." This process of adapting the Creative Curriculum goals, guidelines, and materials to support both the needs of the group and each individual child is a sensitive juggling act.

KEY QUOTE

"It looks easy on paper but it's hard to match the curriculum with each child's DRDP goals and our children's ability levels are so different. We look for small moments to extend each child's learning."

As Alma notes, "It looks easy on paper but it's hard to match the curriculum with each child's DRDP (California's ECE assessment: Desired Results Developmental Profile) goals and our children's ability levels are so different. We look for small moments to extend each child's learning." Alma and her colleagues have found over the years that success comes in extending small moments of observation and support for each child's talents and needs. The teachers add certain words and terms as they see fit in their class discussions, and they are ready to change course and go on a tangent if children have new ideas. For example, one child asked, "Do fruits grow only from trees?" The children thought broccoli was a tree because it has branches and leaves on top. So the teachers found a picture of broccoli to show and after a group discussion, the older children determined that broccoli was not a tree.

Dale Long is another veteran preschool teacher who has adapted his literacy curriculum over the years. Dale has taught preschool children of Color in public schools for 25 years, and is passionate about molding children into lifelong learners and building upon their natural abilities for literacy and social-emotional learning to navigate the world. Dale's approach to curriculum adaptation for young children of Color is based on his deep belief in supporting children's curiosity and self-esteem. Dale believes that in the early stages of creating a meaningful and effective literacy curriculum in preschool, it is critical to help children cultivate a sense of ownership of letters and words. For example, his approach to literacy teaching is founded upon his children's fascination that letters represent words and that there are meanings behind the letters. The children also begin to take pride when they first realize that a letter in their name represents the child – they learn to "own" that single letter.

In this organic and emergent process in Dale's classroom, children learn to recognize more letters in their name until they recognize their entire name, and then they find those letters in other words in books and in print around the classroom. Once they grasp that concept, they learn to see that words can form phrases and sentences. Dale nurtures this concept through frequent read-alouds, book sharing and book browsing, and dictation. In dictation, Dale writes down children's words to accompany their drawings, and then he and the child read back the dictation together. Dale believes in the process of children learning to associate words with pictures, a parallel developmental process to the use of picture books in his daily read-alouds and informal book browsing.

Dale strongly believes in honoring and supporting the literacy strengths and understanding of young children of Color.

> They might not be as exposed to literacy as much as some of their more well-off counterparts, and so I need to be more creative, find literacy activities and strategies that they can relate to. My curriculum builds off a print-rich environment, and when children of Color see a print-rich environment they extend their learning with me, on their own, and with their peers. I build my teaching strategies on my children's resilience and interest to learn. I provide access to more word play and word meanings, story time, library, books sent home, name charts, labels for different classroom areas – I build upon what they have and learn at home and I don't rely on what they may not have been exposed to.

Dale is constantly searching for new literacy ideas and practices that build upon his children's enthusiasm for the power of literacy as a symbol system, for their interest in owning letters and words, and for using their funds of knowledge to access the literacy curriculum and knowledge.

KEY QUOTE

"I build my teaching strengths on my children's resilience and interest to learn."

Over the last several years, Dale has added new instructional ideas such as sentence strips and journal dictation. He writes the children's names at one end of the sentence strip, and then the children write if they can; if not, Dale writes dots to connect and he sits with the children and then later encourages them to write their names. Dale dates the children's first attempt to write their names, takes photographs of the attempt, and stores it in his iPad so he can have a dated record.

Dale uses journals once a week, in which children try to write words around the room and write their name. If he has adult volunteers, Dale also organizes small groups of children to work with the volunteers who encourage the children to draw and write letters. They talk about the journals in the small group and the children get a chance to talk about what they've written (scribbled or written conventionally) and what they've drawn. For read-alouds, Dale has introduced *Kamishibai*, a traditional Japanese wooden box or small theater in which cards are read from behind the theater and children view the pictures in the front. Dale has noticed that his children are fascinated with his dramatic reading of the books, and the visual, performative, and dramatic nature of the theater holds their attention over long periods of time.

Professional Inquiry and Educational Change

An individual and institutional devotion to the process of professional inquiry renews educators' passion and talents for literacy teaching and provides an ongoing collaborative forum and structure for increasing our knowledge of strength-based literacy education.

Attention to Theory and Professional Growth

Ambreen Khawaja is a veteran early childhood teacher and educator who currently serves a site supervisor at the large Head Start preschool where Mr. Jon, Alma, and Hannah teach. Ambreen believes in instilling a knowledge of and passion for educational theory in all of the teachers at her site, as it provides a conceptual foundation for understanding and supporting the literacy talents of children of Color and their families. Ambreen places special emphasis on the work of Lev Vygotsky (1978) and his ideas on socially scaffolded learning, the zone of proximal development, and the value of linking thought, language, and play in mixed-aged settings. Vygotsky's ideas helped Ambreen envision language and literacy-rich environments for her site, and to focus using multiple modalities and the full range of children's literacy talents. In her long tenure at the school, Ambreen has added professional development on the Reggio Emilia approach as well as learning stories, which she believes provide inspirational teaching and learning through experience and literacy-rich activities and projects. Much of this work has been facilitated by outside consultants, and for this kind of professional growth to take root and flourish over time, Ambreen continues to look for new ways for teachers to take on new roles and identities as teacher inquirers in collaboration with colleagues and families.

KEY IDEA

Long-lasting and meaningful professional growth in the area of literacy education must involve teachers and administrators who take on new roles and identities as inquirers.

As an administrator, Ambreen has worked to balance achieving high-quality literacy teaching with the Head Start paperwork, regulations, and assessments. She has worked to reduce the paperwork for teachers so they have more time for the children, and is continually looking for to articulate her school's blend of Creative Curriculum with elements of the Project Approach, Reggio Emilia, and learning stories. Of particular current concern for Ambreen is her goal of encouraging more creativity, openness, risk-taking, and critical thinking in the school's literacy program. For instance, Ambreen asked several teachers to form an inquiry group at the school, and the teachers collected and presented their observations and classroom artifacts with colleagues, and created learning stories based on this material. Ambreen sees great potential in this process of documentation and stories, which highlights both state and federal-mandated learning outcomes and tells an organic, holistic story of how a project evolved, as well as what individual students learned by linking content, ideas, language, and literacy. As a more long-term goal, Ambreen wants to connect the learning stories with a Vygotskian framework, and to include families more deeply in the inquiry and reflection process.

Linking Inquiry, Documentation, and Narrative

Isauro Michael Escamilla is a long-time teacher inquirer who has carried a number of inquiry and documentation projects both on his own and with colleagues. I have worked with Isauro and his colleagues over the last several years in a monthly teacher inquiry and reflection group at their preschool. Isauro's inquiry work has deepened and broadened to include new connections among inquiry, reflection, and narrative within the collaborative environment of his school's inquiry group, which I have helped to facilitate over the last several years.

Isauro's insights into the value of stories as a form of professional development and educational change began with his new awareness of the power of stories for children. He sees great value in the stories that children tell us, and to recognize that children tell stories in multiple ways by drawing, painting, building, constructing, recycled paper, or repurposing recycled materials.

Stories help children to express their ideas, and before they read and write they have to explore spoken language; we need to honor that, and not jump into rhyming and other literacy skills. Behind a child's play, scribbles, or hand-made artifacts there's usually an untold story that keen observers can capture to tell, write, and share with children, families, and colleagues, as deemed appropriate but always from a strength-based perspective.

Isauro used to think that children's family stories were not relevant or important in the school setting, but he now values these home stories, which have shown Isauro the importance of no longer making a distinction between home and school literacy learning. The children's stories have also influenced Isauro's inquiry and reflection work in seeing the power of narrative as a tool and medium for professional growth and development.

> I was used to writing anecdotes for maintaining objectivity, but when I discovered that story is a valid form of inquiry, I embraced and switched to visual and written narratives about one child or a small group or the entire class. When I write these stories, I find the value of what children and their families contribute and bring to the classroom, the human and emotional value of their stories.

KEY QUOTE

"I used to write anecdotes for maintaining objectivity, but when I discovered that story is a valid form of inquiry, I embraced and I switched to visual and written narratives about one child or a small group or the entire class. When I write these stories, I find the value of what children and families contribute and bring to the classroom, the human and emotional value of their stories."

Isauro's current interest in learning stories is rooted in his growing awareness of the power of children's stories. He now sees himself as a storyteller in writing and through photographs and short videos that can represent important moments and insights into children's language and literacy learning.

For example, Isauro created one learning story about a child who became fascinated with the word "*frontera*," or border, because of its powerful connections to his family in the U.S. and in Mexico. Taking their cue from the child, Isauro and his colleagues created a series of activities over several days inspired by the child's engagement with this one word. The child didn't know the word in English, but he was talking about it in Spanish, and Isauro wanted to find out from the child's perspective what the word meant to him and his family. In this process of linking inquiry, documentation, and narrative, Isauro and his colleagues have seen new possibilities in their literacy teaching for exploring the social, familial, and political power of words and languages.

Chapter Summary and Reflections

This chapter presented the perspectives, experiences, ideas, and practices of several teachers and administrators of Color who have worked to conceptualize and support the literacy talents of children and families of Color. The educators have all taken different paths in their journey toward understanding and implementing a strength-based literacy curriculum, and have done so in memory and in honor of their own childhoods and early schooling experiences around language and literacy teaching and learning. Some of their perspectives are founded upon the power of linking literacy education with social justice, equity, and educational change within early childhood institutions. Other educators highlight the social and personal connections with children and families of Color, and how these connections help make the children's literacy talents and interests visible and valid. Still other educators emphasize the value of continually tinkering and experimenting with their literacy teaching, and believe in the process of inquiry, documentation, and reflection as an effective pathway to professional growth and development.

TEACHER AND ADMINISTRATOR PERSPECTIVES AND PRACTICES – THEORETICAL LINKS

- *Codes of power* (Lisa Delpit)
- *Dominant participation patterns* (Courtney Cazden and interpreters)
- *Culturally responsive education* (Gloria Ladson-Billings, Mariana Souto-Manning, and others)
- *Multilingualism, multiliteracies, and synergy* (Eve Gregory and colleagues)
- *Inquiry, documentation, reflection, and narrative* (Vivian Paley, Carlina Rinaldi, Margaret Carr, and others)

For instance, Carlos Castillejo and other educators in this chapter highlight the role of *codes of power*, and the importance of recognizing that schools are institutions of power and that we as educators must be cognizant of our control over the languages and literacies of young children and their families. Carlos, for instance, values giving children the power and the words to speak and for their voices to be heard and their identities to be made visible. Carlos's awareness helps us conceptualize, plan, and implement literacy curriculum that shifts some of the control over languages and literacies from school to the children and families.

The educators in this chapter are also aware of the value of recognizing and changing *dominant participation patterns* in preschool classrooms. For example, Amanda Ibarra recognizes the challenges in the time-honored tradition of whole-class read-alouds in preschools, which can prove problematic developmentally for a large group of three- to five-year-old children who speak a range of languages. So Amanda has worked to supplement and extend the whole-class read-alouds with small-group work where she and her colleagues can fine-tune their questions, prompts, vocabulary, and activities about books and stories to connect with individual children's literacy needs, talents, and interests.

Culturally responsive teaching, a large umbrella framework, is difficult to break down and put into practice in preschool literacy education. The educators in this chapter engage in this process by keeping in mind the ultimate goals of learning to see children's literacy talents, and of finding new ways to make these talents visible and to contribute to the overall literacy success of the classroom, school, and program. For instance, in her work with children and families of Color, Maria Sujo learned to see that these children may bring "a different skill set" to preschool literacy learning, a repertoire of funds of knowledge with its own power, value, and validity. Prenties Brown developed a deep belief in the power of culturally relevant children's books that affirm children's racial, cultural, and familial identities, and also provide content and stories that support and extend children's own interests as linked with their identities.

New language learners learn about languages, literacies, and their social and cultural worlds through mix-aged and intergenerational learning, and rely on *synergy*, a reciprocal learning process between learners who take on teaching roles. In using repeated readings of books and stories in his classroom, Mr. Jon uses a step-like progression of reading where he first emphasizes only the book's visuals, then the book's text and meaning, and then finally encourages the children to share and "read" the books to each other, essentially taking on co-teaching roles with each other.

A dedication to infusing literacy teaching with the process of *inquiry, documentation, and reflection* provides an ongoing path for professional development and growth, and new lenses and tools for recognizing and supporting the literacy talents and interests of young children of Color. When the role of *narrative* is added to this process, as in the use of learning stories from New Zealand, then children's stories, educators' stories, and families' stories become inter-connected, and new home-school-community vantage points and connections are made to support children's literacy learning. Isauro Michael Escamilla, for instance, has worked with his colleagues and with me in our monthly inquiry group to document children's stories, and to use the framework of learning stories to reflect upon and make visible children's literacy abilities, interests, and needs. I discuss more fully the role of inquiry and reflection in literacy teaching in Chapter 6.

END-OF-CHAPTER REFLECTIONS

- What new ideas do you now have for deepening and extending your *image of the literacy talents* of young children of Color? Which perspectives and ideas from this chapter influenced your new image of children's talents and why?
- Which ideas and practices to make children's *literacy talents and abilities more visible* in preschools do you find most appealing? What instructional changes might you make to give children's ideas, achievements, questions, insights, and creations *greater visibility* in the classroom and school?
- What new ideas do you have for deepening your literacy teaching in connection with *culturally responsive teaching*? For instance, do you have new ideas for books to read and share, and new possibilities for structuring your book and story prompts and questions to promote increased social and cultural connections to books?
- How might you now either begin or strengthen your work as a teacher inquirer, and link *inquiry, documentation, and reflection* to strengthen your knowledge of ways to support the literacy talents of children of Color? How do you now see the role of narrative and learning stories to extend your knowledge of a strength-based approach to literacy education?

SECTION II

Achieving High Levels of Excellence

4

THE POWER OF CHILDREN'S LITERATURE – BOOK SELECTION AND TEACHING STRATEGIES

OPENING REFLECTIONS

- What personal memories of your childhood and early schooling influence how and why you select and use children's literature?
- Are there a few favorite books that you use that you feel exemplify your vision and philosophy for a strength-based approach to literacy education?
- What are three of your most important instructional goals for selecting children's literature to support the literacy interests and talents of young children of Color?
- Do you have any goals for strengthening your use of children's literature with young children of Color and their families?

In this chapter, I present several foundational ideas and strategies for selecting children's literature and implementing reading strategies to support the literacy talents of young children of Color. This chapter focuses on books and strategies that I used in supporting children's early interest in and understanding during whole-class read-aloud sessions. In the next chapter, I present my work on a small-group format focusing on children's dictation, drawing, and early writing. In both of these chapters, I provide illustrative examples from my teaching, many of which I documented in my reflective teaching journal. As you read the material, please also keep in mind the relevant theory and practice from Chapter 1, the families' literacy beliefs and ideas and practices from Chapter 2, and the perspectives and practices of the educators profiled in Chapter 3.

The Special Role of Children's Literature

Traditional "progressive" philosophies and approaches to preschool learning and growth continue to emphasize playful and discovery-based experiences with oral stories, storytelling, and books. At the same time, in large part due to increased literacy expectations in public primary and elementary schools, as well as a realization in selected research and policy that discovery-based literacy education does not benefit all children equally, an emphasis on specific literacy skills and knowledge now plays an important role in early childhood literacy education.

In light of increased literacy expectations and assessments in many preschool programs and curricular approaches, I raise three important questions:

1. What is the role of children's literature in a strength-based view of literacy education for children of Color?
2. How can we integrate the use of literature for children's enjoyment, cultural affirmation, academic achievement, content knowledge, and community building?
3. How can we do all this while still giving pedagogical space and time to the developmental needs and learning trajectories of individual children?

Fortunately, the arena of children's literature is an important aspect of preschool literacy education where educators can find both professional satisfaction, curricular choice, and instructional strength. Over the last 20 years, there has been a steady growth in the quantity and quality of multicultural, multilingual children's books to engage teachers, children, and families in the joy and wonders of words, languages, worldviews, and stories. When used with pedagogical intention and instructional integration that accounts for key elements from research (see e.g. Chapter 1) and the perspectives of educators and families of Color (see e.g. Chapters 2 and 3), children's literature can promote children's sense of self-worth, provide information/inspiration, and nurture a sense of pleasure (Brinson, 2012). When thoughtfully used in conjunction with engaging and child-centered activities, children's literature can also support the more technical aspects of reading and writing knowledge and development for children of Color. These areas include children's emerging concepts about print, book language, phonemic awareness, letter and sound identification, early word identification, rhyming, dictation, word meaning and word sense, early writing, and inference- and hypothesis-making.

KEY IDEA

High-quality multicultural and multilingual children's literature inspires joy, cultivates the imagination, and also supports children's engagement with the foundations for learning to read.

Selecting High-Quality Children's Books

Years ago when I was a novice teacher, I often made two classic mistakes in book selection. First, I used children's books and read-alouds as a management tool to help children become focused and calm their energy and excitement. Second, I took a random book from the book shelf and read it to the class without any prior thought as to why I chose the book, how I wanted to read the book, or what I hoped we would gain from the book experience as a classroom community of learners, readers, writers, and critics.

Over the years, I've learned that selecting high-quality multilingual and multicultural books takes a good deal of time, energy, research, and a healthy measure of trial and error. There are several key elements for selecting effective books for whole-class and small-group read-alouds and for children's informal individual and peer-to-peer book browsing and sharing (Figure 4.1).

These elements include print and digital books that are child responsive and developmentally engaging, culturally responsive and sustaining, feature engaging visuals and a sense of aesthetics, and emphasize intriguing vocabulary that spark's children's curiosity and imagination about words and their meanings in text and in the world.

KEY IDEA

Effective book selection includes print and digital books that are child responsive and developmentally engaging, culturally responsive and sustaining, feature engaging visuals and a sense of aesthetics, and emphasize intriguing vocabulary that spark children's curiosity and imagination about words and their meanings in text and in the world.

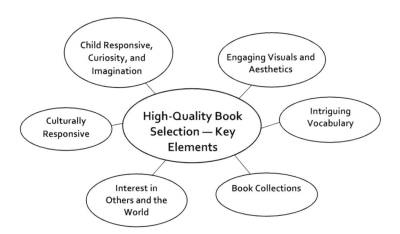

FIGURE 4.1 High-Quality Book Selection – Key Elements

Child Responsive and Developmentally Engaging

One key criterion in the careful selection of books to support the literacy talents of preschool children of Color involves books that are child responsive, and speak to children's developmental talents and needs. Examples of child responsive and developmentally engaging books include *Bear and Hare: Snow!* (Gravett, 2014) and *Bear and Hare Go Fishing* (Gravett, 2015), *Dinner at the Panda Palace* (Calmenson, 1995), *What a Tale* (1986) and *Whose Shoes?* (Wildsmith, 1984), *Neighborhood Mother Goose* (Crews, 2003), Jerry Pinkney's *The Lion & the Mouse* (2009), and *The Bus for Us* (Bloom, 2013). These are books that preschoolers immediately form a bond with, delighting in the identifiable action and plot, the appealing visuals (*Whose Shoes?* and *The Lion & the Mouse* are both wordless books), the engaging characters and objects, the content that reflects their lives and interests, and the approachable language.

For example, in the *Bear and Hare* series, young children enjoy the mix of spare text and appealing visuals and the humorous interactions and predicaments that feature the entertaining duo of *Bear and Hare*. Children find the characters and the storyline funny and engaging, and love predicting and then remembering each unexpected turn of events as we turn a page. For instance, in *Bear and Hare Go Fishing*, children love to anticipate and then identify each item that Bear catches in sequence with his fishing pole – a boot, a frog, and finally a fish, just as Bear is so tired of not catching a fish that he's falling asleep from boredom. And when individual children form these connections with these and other child responsive books, then they become class favorites and are enjoyed and relished communally.

Once these books are introduced and reread several times, children learn to anticipate and predict important elements of the books. For instance, as I read several of Nina Crews's *Neighborhood Mother Goose* rhymes over several weeks, the children learned to memorize and predict the rhymes. As children become more familiar with certain books, I find it effective to introduce one or two additional new books during each read-aloud session, which results in a continual cycle of reading and discussing both familiar and unfamiliar books. This process allows children to practice and solidify what they know from known books, and apply this knowledge to new and unfamiliar books. For example, in one read-aloud session, I reread *The Neighborhood Mother Goose* and *Dinner at the Panda Palace*, and then I introduced two new wordless books, *What a Tale* and *Whose Shoes?*

Reflective Teaching Journal – January 7

We started by rereading several of Nina Crews's Mother Goose rhymes that I had enlarged at a Xerox store onto large sheets, which Amanda [the head teacher] displayed in the classroom. More of the children are remembering the rhymes, and more are predicting rhyming words. We also reread *Dinner at the Panda Palace*, and now more children are identifying the animals and remembering the number of animals in each group that enters the restaurant on each page. For new books, we read *What a Tale* and also *Whose Shoes?*, both by Brian Wildsmith, and the children very much enjoyed both, guessing the name of the shoes in *Whose Shoes?* and matching the tails in *What a Tale* with the corresponding animals shown at the end. *What a Tale* also proved popular with a few children during our small-group work in the children's personal journals that followed our whole-class read-aloud.

An important common denominator, then, in using familiar and new books is this foundation of using books in which preschool children can immediately find social, communal, and literary connections that build and strengthen over time.

Culturally Responsive and Sustaining

> ### KEY IDEA
>
> Culturally responsive and culturally sustaining children's books speak to children, educators, and families in deep ways that resonate with time-honored cultural beliefs, practices, values, and dreams.

A second important criterion pertains to books that children find responsive to their social, cultural, familial, and communal identities, as well as to their evolving literacy identities at school and at home. Examples of culturally responsive books that children are drawn to include Jacqueline Woodson's (2018) *The Day You Begin*, Christopher Myers's (2000) *Wings*, Grace Lin's (1999) *The Ugly Vegetables*, Matt De la Peña's (2017) *Last Stop on Market Street*, Duncan Tonatiuh's (2011) *Diego Rivera*, Pat Mora's (2009) *Gracias/Thanks*, Jerry Pinkney's (2000) *Aesop's Fables*, Benji Davies' (2014) *The Storm Whale* and its sequel *The Storm Whale in Winter* (2017), Nina Crews's (2003) *The Neighborhood Mother Goose, Below* (2006) and its sequel *Sky High* (2010), *I'll Catch the Moon* (Crews, 1996) and *You Are Here* (Crews, 1998), and Langston Hughes and Charles Smith's (2009) *My People*.

For example, children love Nina Crews's *You Are Here* and *I'll Catch the Moon*, two stories featuring children of Color that are set in urban landscapes and have just the right dose of imagination and adventure for preschoolers. In *You Are Here*, two girls are bored on a rainy day and decide to entertain themselves by playing an imaginative game inside. In *I'll Catch the Moon*, a young girl looks out onto the nighttime cityscape from her bed, and takes off on a fantastic journey in space. These books, as with most of Nina Crews's books, depict children of Color engaged in adventures and journeys that draw upon their funds of knowledge and familial, communal, and cultural capital. Crews's books highlight children of Color as strong characters who take action and solve problems, such as finding a lost toy in *Below* (2006), and who are valued members of their families, neighborhoods, and communities.

It is also effective to use culturally responsive books along with physical gestures and oral language discussion, a sensory and linguistic integration that pulls children further into the story as a community of learners.

Reflective Teaching Journal – April 14

We reread Nina Crews's *I'll Catch the Moon*, and we again acted out holding the small moon, putting it into our [pretend] pockets, and making a ladder to climb and climb to reach the moon, just as we had done the previous week. We talked about whether the moon would be larger or smaller if you were close to it. There was some disagreement!

Culturally responsive and sustaining books are not only those books that children of Color recognize and are familiar with in terms of content, visuals, character, and language, but also other books that offer children new opportunities for expanding cultural, social, and literary boundaries. For instance, I introduced the renowned African-American author and artist Jerry Pinkney's *Aesop's Fables* as a new book genre from a different part of the world and historical time period.

Reflective Teaching Journal – April 14

I introduced Jerry Pinkney's *Aesop's Fables* for the first time and we read three fables. I first explained that fables are short stories that include a moral or a lesson. I read the fables and stopped to explain certain vocabulary that was difficult and unusual such as "merry," which I defined as happy, in the "Grasshopper and the Ants." The children were eager to predict certain aspects of the fables, for instance, when I paused and asked how the mouse might free the lion, and then I read that the mouse freed the lion by gnawing the net with his teeth. The children were eager to guess the morals, and were getting the idea of a lesson learned from this new genre.

While Jerry Pinkney's *Aesop's Fables*, as well as his wordless *The Lion & the Mouse* (2009), do not depict children of Color, Pinkney is a consummate author and artist of Color whose books speak powerfully to children of varied histories, cultures, world views, and life lessons. When I use his books, I talk about Pinkney's work as an author and illustrator of Color, and show children pictures of Pinkney, his work, and his studio (see www.jerrypinkneystudio.com/).

Engaging Visuals and Aesthetics

Children of Color are also drawn to books with engaging visuals and aesthetics that speak to their social, cultural, communal, and historical traditions, values, and practices. Nina Crews's books blend photographs and computer-generated images of children in familiar urban spaces engaged in child- and family-oriented activities such as gardening and playing, as well as the depiction of fantastic and imaginative worlds that exist with children's inner worlds. Jerry Pinkney's books are masterpieces of color and movement and detail. As I show children the visuals in Pinkney's wordless *The Lion & the Mouse*, and we try to co-narrate a possible storyline, the children love to observe the small details of setting, action, and movement in the illustrations, which build anticipation as the children wait for the final act of friendship between the two characters. Children also love to play with the aesthetics of the physical properties of books. They enjoy putting their hands through the hole on the cover of *Bear and Hare: Snow!* (2014), opening the flaps in *Shh! (Don't Tell Mr. Wolf!)* (McNaughton, 1999), and flipping the pages vertically in Eric Carle's *Opposites* (Carle, 2007). Repeated exposure to books with engaging and varied visuals and aesthetics not only helps children become connoisseurs of books but provides them with potential models for their own artwork connected with books.

When this groundwork of engagement is cultivated in whole-class read-aloud sessions, books with appealing visuals also promote a high level of interest for book browsing and discussion when I work with small groups of children.

Reflective Teaching Journal – October 16

I also read with Carlos and Juan after the whole-group read-aloud. We read all four books that I brought – Benji Davies's *The Storm Whale* (2014), Ruth Brown's *Snail Trail* (2010), Colin McNaughton's *Shh! (Don't Tell Mr. Wolf!)*, and Pat Mora's *Gracias/Thanks* (2009). I asked questions primarily about the visuals to keep them engaged – can you find ___? Where is ____? For instance, we looked for the six cats in *The Storm Whale*, and the boys eagerly counted all six cats on one double-spread page. Carlos also eagerly and carefully counted all 61 bees in one picture of *Gracias/Thanks*.

The small details in the visuals in Benji Davies's *The Storm Whale* and Pat Mora's *Gracias/Thanks* sparked the children's interest in counting, resulting in the children's effort to count all the cats in *The Storm Whale* and all the bees in *Gracias/Thanks*. The built-in element of animals to count promoted another level of child-centered social engagement with the visuals of the books.

Intriguing Vocabulary

KEY IDEA

High-quality children's literature expands and deepens children's interest in and curiosity about new words, their meanings, and the particular sense that words make in the specific context in which they are placed in a phrase, sentence, or longer stretch of text.

Preschool children learn new vocabulary, both new word meanings and the sense of words in context, through engaging and inviting oral stories, and fiction and nonfiction books. The "meaning" of a word is more closely linked to how a dictionary will define a word, while the "sense" of a word is more closely connected to its specific linguistic context in a phrase or sentence or longer stretch of text. Put another way, high-quality children's literacy can introduce children to the semantic clues (or the meaning behind words), as well as to lexical clues (or words and their immediate linguistic context) (Gregory, 2008). Children need access to both types of clues to gain a deeper understanding of the subtleties of word meaning and how a particular word can be used in varied contexts.

There are many high-quality children's books that promote important connections between word meanings and word sense. Eric Carle's *Opposites* provides a challenging read and discussion of opposite words with visuals that are not all what they seem at first glance. The word "young" is paired with the depiction of a boy drawing, and then lifting the flap of the book, the word "old" is paired with the picture of an old man drawing with the same writing tool. I have found that children at first are unaware that the opposite of "young" can be "old," which challenges them to consider how the illustrations help with the word meanings, and we discuss whether an additional opposite pair could also be "boy" and "man," which is plausible, too.

Reflective Teaching Journal – December 10

We started by rereading Eric Carle's *Opposites*. Most of the children remembered the opposites, and when I asked if the boy for the word "young" might be the opposite of the old man for the word "old," they agreed. Sara said, "I didn't know caterpillars turned into snakes" (the next page after young/old) for the page of "short" with a caterpillar and the hidden flap of a snake and the word "long." I agreed! Dominique had said "big" for "long," and I said that something can be long and big at the same time.

In Brian Wildsmith's wordless *Whose Shoes?*, the children engage in the vocabulary as a problem-solving process of identifying the shoes in the book, some of which can have multiple "names." The first shoes depicted could be "sneakers" or "high-tops" or "running shoes" or "basketball shoes." The second shoes depicted can be "fancy shoes" or "dress shoes" or even "clown shoes," which are actually depicted on the next page.

Reflective Teaching Journal – December 12

We started by rereading Brian Wildsmith's *Whose Shoes?* The children thought the ice skate was a roller skate, and I added actions for each shoe this time, such as "Let's put on our ice skates and skate" to add physical gestures to link the visuals with actions and words.

In Suzanne Bloom's *The Bus for Us*, the children are challenged to identify each new vehicle about to appear on the next page, and are provided a small clue as part of each vehicle peeks out from the previous page. A taxi is followed by a "tow truck," and then a "fire engine" (which children often identify as a "fire truck"), an "ice-cream truck," a "garbage truck" (and I note that it can also be called a "sanitation truck"), then a "backhoe" (which the children call a "back digger" or "a digger thing"), until the big yellow bus finally arrives. In these ways, the children use their own approximations for understanding the specific vocabulary.

Reflective Teaching Journal – December 12

We then read a new book, *The Bus for Us*. The children needed help identifying a few of the vehicles such as the backhoe, which one child called a "back digger." Tony [Maria Carriedo's son mentioned in Chapter 2] predicted the ice cream truck, from the hint of the truck peeking out from the prior page; in general, the class loved the idea of communally predicting what vehicle might come next and identifying each vehicle.

Other books offer different possibilities for exploring word meanings, as in Leo Lionni's (1967) *Frederick*.

Reflective Teaching Journal – December 12

We read a new book, Leo Lionni's *Frederick*, and we read the first story, "Frederick." This was the longest story we have read all year, but the children seemed engaged, and we acted out some of the actions of the mice and of Frederick, such as "gathering" the sunrays and the colors and the words. I asked the class to think of words from outside, from around the room, from what they ate for breakfast, and we scooped up the words. We even cleared our throats to parallel Frederick's action. I will reread this story again next week and add more comprehension prompts.

In this story, "Frederick," we pretend to "gather" sunrays, colors, and words, just as Frederick does. The word "gather" is not a word that most preschoolers have heard, and Lionni's use of this word in "Frederick" gives the story a poetic and almost metaphoric feel. Further, as we gather the sunrays, colors, and words, the children participate with Frederick in planning for change and adaptation – "I gather sunrays for the cold dark days," "I gather colors for the winter is gray," and "I am gathering words" for "the winter days are long and many, and we'll run out of things to say" (Lionni, 1967). The children's engagement with these words and this literary language provides an elevated and more sophisticated examination of words in their specific contexts; Frederick's gathering of colors gives the language a sense of poetry and moves the plot along through intentional word choice.

Digital Books and Stories

KEY IDEA

Digital books and stories have the potential to complement and extend children's experiences with conventional books through a different form of social interaction around text and visual, and they offer new possibilities for student control and re-enactment of the reading process.

I also worked with the children using digital stories from an online, open source platform (https://libris.app/books) that features books from around the world read by a digitized voice. Working in small groups, a format that I discuss later in this chapter and more fully in the next chapter, the children themselves select stories to read from a selection of over 75 books. I sometimes allow the children to press the tracking pad on my laptop to advance each page of the stories as we listen and look at the visuals. Since the children and I advance each page, we are free to stop at any point in the story, and to highlight and discuss any story element or visual as we wish, much as we did in using the paper books.

KEY IDEA

The use of digital stories can allow for great flexibility of book selection by children themselves, and provide expanded opportunities for peer-to-peer and child-to-adult discussion and oral language use about books, stories, characters, and visuals.

There are a few important benefits of using the digitized books in the same open, communal manner as our shared book-reading of the paper books. First, the initial display of the digital books on the screen allows children to look at the covers of dozens of books, which enables them to recognize familiar and favorite books that they often like to reread and also to search for new books that they might want to read. I also encourage children to listen and look at the books and decide on books to read on their own; sometimes, one child at a time chooses a book for the computer to read, and sometimes they all agree on one or more books to read, and I encourage the children to shake hands and agree on their selections and the order in which they will be read. In essence, this process gives over a bit of the read-aloud control to the children as I step back from my usual read-aloud role.

Second, the digital application highlights each word in a color as it is read out loud by the computer, reinforcing word-for-word reading and tracking, as well as left-to-right progression, helpful elements for reinforcing concepts of print. Third, since the computer-generated voice reads the book, it is possible for the children and me to talk over the narration to refer to an aspect of the book and also to point to objects or actions as the book is read. Fourth, the computer-generated narration also allows children to talk over the narration and to converse with each other while the story is read and there is no need for an adult to be present to support the reading. For example, Ariadna, Veronica, and I listened to *The Dancer's Tale* (Cutler, De Klerk, & Pita, 2014), which many children loved, and the two children held brief conversations at different points of the book reading.

ARIADNA: They're (two main characters) married.
VERONICA: I like the purple one (dancer).
ARIADNA: He's a boy. Not a girl.
VERONICA: Is that a boy or a girl?

In this instance, the opportunity to problem-solve the characters' gender identities as the computer read the story out loud allowed me to listen in on the children's conversation, and to have the opportunity to write it down in my reflective teaching journal for later reflection.

The computer-generated narration also enables me to help the children dramatize certain aspects of the digital stories, and as the children and I make physical movements that mirror the action in the stories, we all become more engaged with the story. For example, we listened to and looked at the digital story *Tortoise Finds His Home* (Fowler, Coetzer, & Gibbs, 2014), a story about a tortoise who, while looking for his house, befriends several animals who climb onto his shell.

I either paused the digital narration or talked over the narration as I prompted the children to act out specific elements of the story. When the digital application read a sentence on the first page, "He looked into the distance and squinted at the grass" (Fowler et al., 2014, p. 1), I asked the children in my small group to slightly cup their hands above their eyes to shield the sun and to squint, as I moved my hands and squinted with exaggeration. As we did this action together a few times, we looked together in the distance just as the tortoise did. As the tortoise continues on his journey, he meets new animals – first a snail, then a sparrow, a ladybird, and a mouse – and we heralded the arrival of each new animal by dramatizing some aspects of each animal. We moved two of our fingers very slowly to mimic the pace of a snail, flapped our wings like the sparrow, pretended to place a tiny ladybird in our outstretched palms, and to rub our imaginary whiskers for the mouse. Not needing to hold a book or devote my attention to reading the text, the digital stories in the small-group format enabled me to have an increased measure of physical and vocal freedom to interact with the children, and for the children to increase their interaction with me and each other as they sensed that they were not interrupting my narration.

Key Instructional Elements

There are several important instructional elements for supporting and showcasing how and why preschool children of Color interact with and learn from high-quality children's books.

KEY IDEA

> The use of high-quality books needs to be intentional and planned, based on both the interests and talents of children and adults in preschool classrooms, and nurtured as the foundation for a classroom community of evolving critics, readers, writers, and thinkers.

Whole-Class Read-Alouds

Whole-class read-alouds, traditionally more the domain of primary grade classrooms, are now quite prevalent in preschool classrooms. When done well, they can be a key structure for introducing, reinforcing, and extending children's understanding of and interactions with children's books. There are several important elements in effective whole-class read-alouds (Figure 4.2):

• Conduct read-alouds a few times each day and allow for varied seating and participation arrangements

- Feature a lively and engaging adult reading style, voice, and presence
- Use high-quality child and culturally responsive books of varied genres and authors that engage both adults and children
- Maintain a continual cycle of familiar and unfamiliar books
- Build on children's imagination and curiosity
- Use selected prompts for discussion and comprehension

There is always the danger that whole-class read-alouds become stale and routinized, and it is important that our passion for and knowledge of high-quality books and the forms of classroom discourse that we employ during read-alouds remain fresh and relevant for ourselves and for the children.

Whole-class read-alouds are also an important way to add a layer of classroom community and solidarity, a key force in promoting social, cultural, intellectual capital within the communal setting of book reading, sharing, and discussion. In this sense, all children are viewed as competent and active listeners, contributors, and problem-solvers, and this spirit and intention can carry over to other areas of the literacy curriculum. The goal of literacy as community is enhanced, as mentioned earlier, when we avoid viewing read-alouds primarily as a time for children to be quiet and listen. When read-alouds are seen primarily as passive listening, then compliance of young children's bodies and minds becomes the main focus rather than active engagement, theorizing, enjoyment, and the co-production of new, shared knowledge for the benefit of the classroom community.

As noted in Figure 4.2, there are several layers in read-alouds that promote children's social engagement and literacy learning. I now pay particular attention to building on children's curiosity and imagination and the use of specific teacher prompts for discussion, problem-solving, and comprehension.

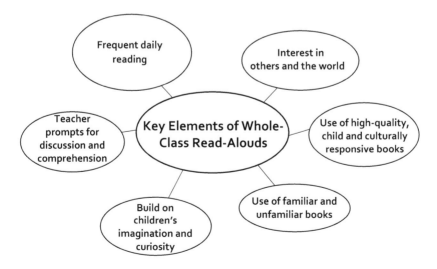

FIGURE 4.2   Key Elements of Whole-Class Read-Alouds

Building on Children's Curiosity and Imagination

We know that curiosity is critical for intellectual development (Engel, 2011), that imagination and story are intimately linked (Egan, 1989), and that the imagination is connected with transformative interactive experiences and social change (Fettes, 2013).

KEY IDEA

Young children connect in powerful ways with high-quality, responsive literature through their imagination and sense of curiosity. It is a primary cognitive, social, and cultural pathway for entering the symbolic story world as if it were real and in the moment of human experience.

When we cultivate and nurture children's sense of curiosity and imagination around high-quality children's books, we support a crucial pathway for children to connect with books, stories, and each other. As mentioned earlier, Nina Crews's (1998) *You Are Here* is a story about two child characters using their imagination to fight the boredom of staying inside on a rainy day, and they go on a fanciful adventure.

Reflective Teaching Journal – March 24

I read Nina Crews's (1998) *You Are Here*, and I explained how Nina Crews makes her books from photographs that she manipulates on a computer. Exavier said that the girls in the story are using their "imagination" for their game, and another student said that the checkers were "poker chips."

Exavier recognizes the imaginative nature of the narrative as described in the text and visuals in Nina Crews's (1998) *You Are Here*, which, like all of her books, depicts young children of Color engaging in daily activities in home and community that children can readily identify with. There is a level of social and cultural comfort and familiarity in Crews's stories that provide an inviting platform for engaging children's sense of imagination and curiosity about story worlds.

There is also the additional element of children's imagination and curiosity as connected to the language of storybooks and to the language of children's lives and experiences. For instance, as I read one of the fables in *Frederick's Fables* with the children, Carlos and Preeya each had a spontaneous vocabulary connection to the process of the chameleon character changing colors.

Reflective Teaching Journal – March 24

I counted the stories we had read so far in *Frederick's Fables* and announced that we have read ten stories, and then I read "A Color of His Own," a story about a chameleon changing colors. Carlos said that chameleons change colors because they want to "camouflage" themselves, and Preeya said that they want to "blend in."

Carlos and Preeya readily enter the magical and imaginative world of Leo Lionni's (1997) *Frederick's Fables*, and offered their own interpretations of how and why chameleons change colors. In effect, they showcase their curiosity about story action and character through the lens of academic vocabulary and within the specifics of our word meaning and word sense work from the previous ten stories in *Frederick's Fables*.

Interest in Others and the World

Children also engage with books that entice them into making new connections with others and the world.

KEY IDEA

High-quality and engaging children's books not only promote opportunities for children to draw upon their funds of knowledge but also entice and support children to expand and deepen this knowledge as linked with classroom and school discourse patterns and expectations.

These and other books encourage children to think and feel beyond themselves and to make connections to new physical environments and social contexts.

For instance, in Benji Davies's *The Storm Whale* (2014) and then continuing in its sequel, *The Storm Whale in Winter* (2017), children are drawn to the main child character, Noi, who discovers a small whale on the beach where he lives. I used a range of prompts to deepen our connections with the story's main predicament, for instance – how is Noi, who is home alone when he finds the whale, going help the whale survive?

Reflective Teaching Journal – October 16

I read *The Storm Whale* by Benji Davies to the whole class. As I read, I used a range of prompts to pull the children into the story world:

- I read a sentence from the text and paused before the last word – "It was a little whale washed up on the _____" and one child said "beach" while another said "sand."
- I asked the class if the whale needed to be in water to survive (the children agreed).
- Later in the book, the text reads: ("Noi often thought about the storm whale. He hoped that one day, soon . . ."), and I pointed to the page that shows two fins coming out of the water and into the air, and I asked, "Who might these two fins belong to?"

On other occasions, children reflected on specific aspects of the social and physical environments in the story. Tashawn noted that it was "not safe" for Noi to be home alone (The text reads: "He [his dad] wouldn't be home again until dark"). Other children predicted that Noi's dad would be mad when he saw the whale in the bathtub (The text reads: "Noi was worried that his dad would be angry about having a whale in the bath"). When children are presented with story predicaments and story lines that appeal to children's social, cultural, and epistemological interest in the world and others, the story world becomes the classroom world.

Small-Group Book Browsing and Peer-to-Peer Book Sharing

KEY IDEA

Engaging read-alouds are best complemented with small-group experiences with ample peer and adult discussion about stories, text, and visuals.

Whole-class read-alouds allow for engaging discussions and connections with high-quality books, and help nurture a literacy community in the classroom. A small-group format builds on the whole-group read-alouds through several specific elements, which range from opportunities for children to revisit the favorite read-aloud books to peer-to-peer book discussions to extended book reading time with an adult (Figure 4.3).

In this section, I describe a few of these key elements and provide illustrative examples.

Revisiting the Read-Aloud Books

It's most effective when small groups immediately follow the whole-class read-aloud sessions. In this way, a small group of children can carry the books that we've just read to another part of the classroom, and the books and stories remain fresh

FIGURE 4.3 Key Elements in Small–Group Book Browsing

in their minds. I then proceed with a fairly predictable two-step routine. First, I often reread one or two of the books from the read-aloud to the small group, to children in pairs, or with individual children. This usually happens spontaneously as I remember the children's interest in the books during the prior read-aloud, and check in with the children about which books most fully resonated with them. I call the subsequent process of children looking at books on their own or with peers "book browsing" or "book sharing," and each child has their own style and talents for this process. I try to track mentally and also take notes in my reflective teaching journal on each child's preferred style of book browsing and which books they are drawn to, which helps me suggest certain books ("Mariah, I remember you liked this book last week, do you want to read it again?") and their style ("Darius, do you want to read this book with Marta again? You can take turns reading it to each other."). In addition to offering the children the books from our just concluded read-aloud, children know that they can also select books from my bookbag of books that we have read over the last few weeks. In this way, the children have access to both familiar and "new" books, enabling them to revisit books and stories that they know, which is a reassuring base for peer conversation, while the "new" books offer a different sense of anticipation and possibility.

The second step of small-group book sharing and browsing involves the children's personal journals, in which they draw, write, and dictate either about the books they are looking at or any other topics. I thoroughly discuss this second element in Chapter 5.

Opportunities to Practice and Extend

The small-group format enables me to spend more literacy time, energy, and attention with individual or just a few children. It is an important opportunity for me to learn about children's literacy interests and talents in more detail, and to follow up with the children by asking questions, engaging in discussion, and talking about books and stories from their out-of-school lives. The small-group format, in turn, allows the children extended time (they can sit with me and the other children for up to 45 minutes or more if they wish) to practice and extend their interest and knowledge of the read-aloud books. It also allows opportunities for me to follow up on a spontaneous idea or strategy from the read-alouds with the whole class or from my notes about an individual child's interaction with a specific book, author, or genre.

In this way, I can work with the children to focus on a range of literacy elements of our read-aloud books, many of which I have discussed earlier in this chapter – text structure, visuals, an author's style, character traits, plot points, specific vocabulary, rhyming, and sound-symbol correspondence. For example, I read *The Storm Whale* with Beto and Ariadna and we extended our understanding of the size of the whale in the book.

Reflective Teaching Journal – November 30

I read *The Storm Whale* with Beto and Ariadna. I have read this book dozens of times with children both in whole-group and small-group formats over the last few years, though suddenly today Beto, Ariadna, and I all became interested in how long and large the whale looked on one page, and wondered how long it was. I thought it would be valuable for the children to measure the whale on the page, and Ariadna found a ruler. We measured the whale as 13 inches long, which prompted Beto to proclaim, "That's a huge whale."

This kind of extended interaction is difficult to achieve in a whole-group setting, but the small-group format allowed us ample time to discuss the image of the whale in the book, locate a ruler, measure and discuss the whale's length, and engage in a collective effort to extend our engagement with the book.

The small-group time also affords children ample opportunities to read together without adult support, and to employ child responsive and culturally responsive strategies in their interactions and conversations. For example, Jonetta and Alonso were reading *Shh! (Don't Tell Mr. Wolf!)* (McNaughton, 1999) together at our small table. This flap-book was especially popular with the children at the time, and the turn-the-flap features to find the pig hiding from Mr. Wolf delighted the children. After Jonetta and Alonso read it together, taking turns turning the pages and opening the flaps, Jonetta said to Alonso, "This time, read it to yourself." After Alonso read it one time on his own, they both it read together again. Then each child chose a new, different book and read their new book on their own, side by side. They then both returned to reading *Shh! (Don't Tell Mr. Wolf!)* together and took turns saying "no!" when each successive flap did not reveal the hiding pig.

Finally, Alonso continued to read the book on his own several more times until he had been sitting and reading for 40 minutes.

The children's evolving engagement with the small-group format for book browsing and revisiting the read-aloud books also transferred to their dictation and drawing in their personal journals, which I discuss in the next chapter. It is important that the children buy into the premise of revisiting and re-engaging with the books in the small-group format as a social, literary, and cultural foundation or springboard for their conversations and work in their personal journals. For example, on one occasion, Exavier and Lupe were in my small group, and they were starting to look at books and begin their journal drawing. Exavier turned to me and said, "I'm opening the book (*The Bus for Us*) so Lupe can see what to draw." He then turned to Lupe and said, "Look it, Lupe, finally the bus is here" as he turned the page. In effect, Exavier took over my role as both guide to the book's visuals and text, and he did so in a collaborative, socially engaging and supportive manner with Lupe.

Child-Initiated Engagement

The small-group format also encourages children to take the initiative in discussing a book or story with peers and adults, which leads to increased social and literacy engagement. For example, I read *The Storm Whale* with three children in our small groups, and one of the children, Eliana, took the lead in responding to my prompts and interacting with her peers around the book.

ELIANA: (to the two other children in our small group) Guys! You gonna listen to the story? Will the whale say good-bye?

CARA: Good-bye!

ELIANA: Now I got your attention.

DANIEL: Okay, let's read it from the beginning. Ready? (to Eliana, who wanted to help turn the pages) Turn the page. That's right. You have it the right way. Turn the page.

Eliana takes the lead by engaging with her peers to join in the story reading, and I let Eliana turn the first pages.

ELIANA: And say goodbye to mom. There was no whale in the water.

DANIEL: (reading from the book) Noi lived with his dad and six cats. Can you count the cats on your hand?

ELIANA: One, two, three!

DANIEL: Count them on your fingers. One, two, three.

ELIANA: Is that a cat?

DANIEL: Four, five, six. Where? Oh I see a cat in a window, can you find the cat in the window? Okay you see the cat. Turn the page, you got it. (reading) Every day, Noi's dad went to work, and he wouldn't be home again until after dark. Do you see any cats in the house?

ELIANA: Yes.

Eliana counts the cats on her fingers with me and also examines the visuals to identify and count the cats.

DANIEL: (continuing reading) As he got closer, Noi could not believe his eyes! It was a little whale washed up on the (pause) sand. Noi wondered what he should do. He knew that it wasn't good for a whale to be out of the (pause) water. What did he bring?

ELIANA: He's gonna, he's gonna, he's gonna wash him up and put, he's gonna give him water.

DANIEL: I must be quick, he thought. What's he doing to him?

ELIANA: He's gonna push him!

DANIEL: Yeah! Where? Where's he taking the whale? Do you remember?

ELIANA: Yeah, he's gonna, he's gonna go to a . . .

DANIEL: Remember? Where does he put the whale?

ELIANA: He puts him in the bathroom.

DANIEL: Mm-hmm. Is that a good idea?

ELIANA: No.

The chance for extensive adult-to-child and peer-to-peer interaction heightened the children's engagement from the beginning, and helped them become more involved in responding to my prompts and conversing about the plot.

DANIEL: (continuing to read) Somehow Noi kept his secret safe all evening. He even managed to sneak some supper for his whale. (and now adding a question) What's he bringing to the whale?

ELIANA: He's gonna bring it to the fishies.

DANIEL: Yes. (reading) But he knew it couldn't last! (asking the children) Uh-oh! Who found out about the whale now?

ELIANA: He's, um gonna swim with him.

DANIEL: (reading) Noi's dad wasn't angry. He had been so busy he hadn't noticed that Noi was lonely. But he said they must take the whale.

ELIANA: Oh it's raining!

DANIEL: Yeah. (reading) Back to the sea, where it belonged. (I then prompted pretend gestures for everyone to row with their arms.) Ok, get in your rowboat.

ELIANA: (makes a sound)

DANIEL: Can you row? Row, row, row. Can you see the whale?

ELIANA: (makes a sound)

DANIEL: No, you don't have to put your jacket on (Eliana was walking toward her cubby). We'll just pretend.

LEAH: Let me see!

DANIEL: See? There's the whale! (reading) Noi knew it was the right thing to do but it was hard to say goodbye.

ELIANA: Goodbye!

CARA: Goodbye whale!

DANIEL: (reading) He was glad his dad was there with him. Noi often thought about the storm whale.

ELIANA: Where's he?

DANIEL: (reading) He hoped that one day soon, dot dot dot (for . . .)

ELIANA: Where's he?

CARA: He, he, washed.

DANIEL: What's he doing? What's Noi doing?

CARA: He's drawing a, he's drawing a, this!

DANIEL: Yeah, he's making pictures of the whale. (reading) He would see his friend again.

ELIANA: Ba-da-ba-da-ba

CARA: Buh-bye!

DANIEL: Did he see his friend again? Eliana, do you want to walk around and ask the children to say goodbye to the whale? Say, "Say goodbye to the whale!"

ELIANA: Bye whale! (showing the book to the other two children) Say goodbye to the whale!

ELIANA: Goodbye to the whale!

CARA: Hello! Buh-bye!

The permeable boundaries of the small-group reading format allow me to slip in several comprehension prompts, and maintain a more moment-by-moment sense of the children's level of engagement and understanding of the story. The more open-ended boundaries also allow the children themselves to take the initiative in the reading and discussion (such as Eliana) and apply their oral language and social skill set to discussing a book with me and peers.

Chapter Summary and Reflections

This chapter examined important criteria for selecting high-quality books for whole-class read-alouds and small-group book sharing with preschool children of Color. It is important to select books that appeal to and engage children in the world of stories, story elements, problem-solving, vocabulary, word-for-word and left-to-right and return-sweep tracking of words, interpreting visuals, and discussing possible meanings and comprehension connections. The overall goal is to promote an integration of open-ended and structured opportunities for children of Color to showcase their literacy interests, knowledge, and skill set in child responsive and culturally responsive ways.

There are a number of ways that the ideas and strategies from this chapter connect with selected research and theory from Chapter 1. For instance, when we select high-quality children's literature that speaks to children's interests, experiences, and knowledge from home and school, we honor important principles of culturally responsive education (Ladson-Billings, 2009, 2014) and funds of knowledge (Gonzalez, Moll, & Amanti, 2006; Moll, Amanti, Neff, & Gonzalez, 1992). For example, regularly selecting books such as Nina Crews's *You Are Here* and other culturally responsive books sends the daily message that we value books and stories that resonate with the literacy and life interests, experiences, talents, and identities of young children of Color.

Our selection of high-quality books, though, is only as effective as the accompanying participation structures and forms of classroom discourse (Au, 1980, 1993; Cazden, 2001) and conversation that we plan for, enact, and monitor through inquiry and reflection. When we fashion whole-class read-alouds and small-group book reading and sharing formats that provide ample opportunities for children's conversation and problem-solving, then we promote permeable participation boundaries and ample pedagogical space for children to contribute their knowledge, feelings, and thoughts (Dyson, 2016). Further, small-group formats that utilize whole-class read-alouds support children to deepen their literacy engagement and learning in a more intimate setting that allows for more child-to-adult and peer-to-peer conversation and interaction.

For example, in reading *The Storm Whale* in a small-group setting with Eliana and a few other children, the children knew that the small-group format allowed them more physical and social initiative and interaction with the book (to touch the page to count the cats and to touch the whale), more problem-solving opportunities with an adult (as I asked them what Noi planned to do to help the whale), and more peer social interaction around book content (as when Eliana turned to the other children in our small group and said, "Guys! You gonna listen to the story? Will the whale say good-bye?").

The careful planning, implementation, and tinkering with book selection and formats for read-alouds, book browsing, book reading, and discussion also provide small moments of sustained attention to important elements of literacy skills and literary knowledge. For example, the opportunity in small-groups to easily see how I move my finger across the page as I read the text shows the children important features of concepts about print, such as word-for-word tracking and the left-to-right and return-sweep of following the text in English. The use of the digital stories in small-group literacy work also helps young children track the word-by-word highlighting of the text.

There are also important connections to the literacy expectations of families of Color from Chapter 2. For instance, the careful selection of high-quality books and the structuring of whole-class read-alouds and small-group book sharing also align with certain goals for several families. For example, an important element of their aspirations as parents concerns how early literacy learning can influence their children's identities as strong and competent literacy users. The ample opportunities in whole-group and small-group literacy activities as described in this chapter promote a public, communal forum for young children of Color to practice elements of their emerging identities as strong and competent literacy users with each other.

As Jamal and Charemon noted, when their daughter Jamilla was in preschool she "developed a love for learning and words," and Jamilla figured out how reading works by "chipping away" at it. The sustained opportunities in small-group book interactions to focus on key vocabulary, character traits, elements of setting and plot, to make inferences, predict, and problem-solve are important ways for preschool children to "chip away" at literacy engagement and knowledge, and to learn how words, larger chunks of discourse, and visuals work together in concert in high-quality children's books.

Lidia, the parent of second-grader Isaiaa and preschooler Julian, noted how much her children enjoy working and interacting with each other around books and reading at home. Isaiaa and Julian enjoy reading books together, and Julian often listens in when Isaiaa asks Lidia questions about what he is reading for his second-grade class. Lidia also notices that Julian will make a comment or ask a question about books that are a "bit mature for his age," which surprises Lidia and indicates Julian's high level of engagement and problem-solving within the cross-age, communal forum of book reading and sharing at home. So when classroom literacy instruction offers ample child-to-adult and child-to-child oral language and interaction, this provides a social, linguistic, and cultural bridge for children to interact in familiar ways with books, stories, and language.

Shyla, the parent of second-grader Exavier with whom I worked when he was in preschool, also believes that "preschool set the foundation" for Exavier's literacy development. Shyla noted that attention to books, and literacy knowledge embedded in books and stories, helped Exavier transition from preschool book sharing experiences to identifying words and beginning to read in kindergarten, and to his continuing interest in asking questions to deepen his comprehension when he reads with Shyla at home. Exavier also tries to "break down the biggest word" he reads, and if he doesn't know how to decode a word or know its meaning, he and Shyla engage in conversation about the structure of the word and what it might mean from the context. So, when young children regularly engage in jointly constructed activities and conversations around the language and word meaning/sense of high-quality children's books in preschool, this process can parallel and support how Shyla and other families engage their young children in highly interactive, conversant ways at home.

As we move into the next chapter, please keep in mind this chapter's discussion of effective ways to select high-quality children's literature and to organize whole-class read-alouds and small-group book browsing and sharing as discussed in this chapter. The daily integration of child and culturally responsive books with depth of meaning and engaging visuals also entices children into the processes of drawing and dictation, which pull them even closer to showcasing their literacy interests, experiences, and talents. The next chapter, then, describes effective ways to conceptualize and structure small-group work around books, stories, dictation, drawing, conversation, and writing.

END-OF-CHAPTER REFLECTIONS

- Which ideas regarding the selection of high-quality children's literature do you find most appealing from this chapter? How might these ideas fit into your short-term and long-term plans for strengthening your literacy teaching? For instance, are there specific books, authors, and genres from this chapter that you would now like to spend time getting to know?
- Which strategies regarding whole-class read-alouds and small-group book browsing and reading do you find most useful and inspiring? How might these strategies fit into your current or future goals for linking whole-group read-alouds with small-group formats?
- In light of the ideas and examples for using digital books and stories described in this chapter, how might you consider introducing or extending your use of digital books and stories in preschool?
- Overall, how have the ideas and strategies for book selection, read-alouds, and book browsing presented in this chapter expanded the instructional possibilities to showcase and support the literacy talents of young children of Color?

Useful Resources

Au, K. H. (1980). Participation structures in a reading lesson with Hawai'ian children: Analysis of a culturally appropriate instructional event. *Anthropology & Education Quarterly, 11*(2), 91–115.

Au, K. H. (1993). *Literacy instruction in multicultural settings.* New York, NY: Wadsworth Publishing Company.

Bloom, S. (2013). *The bus for us.* Honesdale, PA: Boyds Mill Press.

Brinson, S. A. (2012). Knowledge of multicultural literature among early childhood educators. *Multicultural Education, 12*(2), 30–33.

Bush, G. W. (2001). *No child left behind.* Washington, DC: U.S. Department of Education.

Calmenson, S. (1995). *Dinner at the panda palace.* Boston, MA: Houghton Mifflin.

Carle, E. (2007). *Eric Carle's opposites.* New York, NY: Grosset & Dunlap.

Cazden, C. B. (2001). *Classroom discourse: The language of teaching and learning* (2nd ed.). Portsmouth, NH: Heinemann.

Crews, N. (1996). *I'll catch the moon*. Boston, MA: Harper Collins.

Crews, N. (1998). *You are here*. New York, NY: Greenwillow Books.

Crews, N. (2003). *The neighborhood Mother Goose*. New York, NY: Greenwillow Books.

Crews, N. (2006). *Below*. New York, NY: Henry Holt and Company, LLC.

Crews, N. (2010). *Sky-high guy*. New York, NY: Henry Holt and Company, LLC.

Cutler, S., De Klerk, T. N., & Pita, R. (2014). *A dancer's tale*. Cape Town: Book Dash.

Davies, B. (2014). *The storm whale*. New York, NY: Henry Holt and Company.

Davies, B. (2017). *The storm whale in winter*. New York, NY: Henry Holt and Company.

De la Peña, M. (2017). *Last stop on Market street*. London: Puffin.

Dyson, A. H. (Ed.). (2016). *Child cultures, schooling, and literacy: Global perspectives on composing unique lives*. New York, NY: Routledge.

Egan, K. (1989). *Teaching as storytelling: An alternative approach to teaching and curriculum in the elementary school*. Chicago, IL: University of Chicago Press.

Engel, S. (2011). Children's need to know: Curiosity in schools. *Harvard Educational Review, 81*(4), 625-645.

Fettes, M. (2013). Imagination and experience: An integrative framework. *Democracy and Education, 21*(1), 4.

Fowler, M., Coetzer, K., & Gibbs, D. (2014). *Tortoise finds his home*. Cape Town: Book Dash.

Gravett, E. (2014). *Bear & hare: Snow!* New York, NY: Simon & Schuster Books for Young Readers.

Gravett, E. (2015). *Bear & hare go fishing*. London: Macmillan Children's.

Gregory, E. (2008). *Learning to read in a new language: Making sense of words and worlds* (2nd ed.). Los Angeles, CA: Sage.

Hughes, L., & Smith, C. R. (2009). *My people*. New York, NY: Atheneum Books for Young Readers/Ginee Seo Books.

Jerry Pinkney Studio. (2019). Retrieved from www.jerrypinkneystudio.com/

Ladson-Billings, G. (2009). *The dreamkeepers: Successful teachers of African American children*. San Francisco, CA: John Wiley & Sons.

Ladson-Billings, G. (2014). Culturally relevant pedagogy 2.0: Aka the remix. *Harvard Educational Review, 84*(1), 74–84.

Lin, G. (1999). *The ugly vegetables*. Watertown, MA: Charlesbridge Publishing.

Lionni, L. (1967). *Frederick*. New York, NY: Random House.

Lionni, L. (1997). *Frederick's fables: A treasury of 16 Leo Lionni favorites*. New York, NY: Knopf Books for Young Readers.

Lobel, A. (2004). *The frog and toad collection*. New York, NY: HarperCollins.

McNaughton, C. (1999). *Shh! (Don't tell mister wolf!)*. London: Andersen Press.

Moll, L. C., Amanti, C., Neff, D., & Gonzalez, N. (1992). Funds of knowledge for teaching: Using a qualitative approach to connect homes and classrooms. *Theory Into Practice, 31*(2), 132–141.

Mora, P. (2009). *Gracias-thanks*. New York, NY: Lee & Low Books.

Myers, C. (2000). *Wings*. New York, NY: Scholastic Press.

Pinkney, J. (2000). *Aesop's fables*. New York, NY: SeaStar Books.

Pinkney, J. (2009). *The lion & the mouse*. New York, NY: Little Brown and Books for Young Readers.

Tonatiuh, D. (2011). *Diego Rivera: His world and ours*. New York, NY: Abrams Books for Young Readers.

Wildsmith, B. (1984). *Whose shoes?* Oxford: Oxford University Press.

Wildsmith, B. (1986). *What a tale*. Oxford: Oxford University Press.

Woodson, J. (2018). *The day you begin*. New York, NY: Nancy Paulsen Books.

5

PERSONAL JOURNALS, DRAWING, AND DICTATION – OPPORTUNITIES FOR SYMBOL INTEGRATION AND SOCIAL SUPPORT

OPENING REFLECTIONS

- What do you see as the benefits of personal journals, drawing, and dictation in the literacy learning of preschool children of Color?
- What do you see as the value of children's literature for supporting children's use of personal journals for drawing, conversation, dictation, and early attempts at writing?
- How might you integrate a mix of open-ended, discovery-based learning and more teacher-scaffolded attention to specific literacy skills and knowledge?
- What are effective ways to structure small-group work focused on children's use of personal journals?

The intentional selection of high-quality children's books, the structured use of whole-class read-alouds, and the sensitive organization of small-group book formats provide an important language, literacy, and social foundation for preschool children of Color to showcase and strengthen their talents for drawing and dictation. The steady, daily stream of child responsive and culturally responsive children's books and stories helps us pick and choose those books that are especially well-suited for engaging children in literacy-related activities. Our attention to specific elements of story and language in the whole-class read-alouds can be extended in small groups through the use personal journals, in which we can support children's symbolic and literacy talents and interests through drawing and dictation activities. Drawing provides opportunities for children to make meaningful marks and represent symbolically their ideas, feelings, experience, and knowledge. Dictation allows children to begin to see some of the complicated inter-connections between thought, art, oral language, and written language. Further, since "texts are socially constructed and created or designed from particular perspectives" (Vasquez, 2017, p. 8), the small-group format adds another layer of social interaction, conversation, and community for children to experiment with drawn and written symbols within the company of adults and peers.

KEY IDEA

When we structure small-group opportunities for children to revisit their favorite read-aloud books, we provide a literary and social pathway for children to see themselves as conversational partners, artists, authors, symbol users and producers, and even literary critics.

Personal Journals

I use personal journals for each child in a small-group format immediately following our whole-class read-aloud session. The personal journals consist of blank paper stapled with construction paper to look like a book. Children write their names on their journal cover either on their own or with assistance from me or another child, and this process offers children the chance to sound out their names, to take their journal to their cubby or coat hook and either copy down their name, or show me how their name is written, and we write it together. The children also write a numeral on the cover so that we can track the chronology of their journal work, and the children are proud of how many journals they complete. If used a few times each week, children can easily create over a dozen personal journals by year's end, and if started when they are young preschoolers, they can produce a substantial number of journals over their preschool years before entering transitional kindergarten or kindergarten.

There are several important benefits of personal journals for preschool children that include reconnecting children to the whole-class read-alouds, offering opportunities for drawing, dictation, and drama, and providing an ongoing record of their literacy engagement over time that documents changes in form and content (Figure 5.1). As portable literacy objects, personal journals also further promote a sense of children's inclusion in a literary community. When children are finished with one or more journal entries during a particular small-group time, I often ask children to walk around the classroom and show and discuss their journal entry with other children and adults. This enables children to receive additional

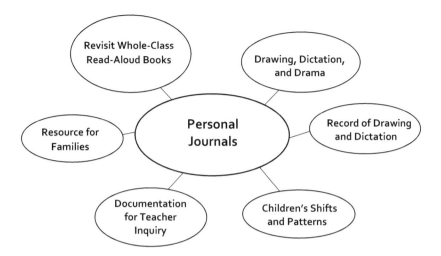

FIGURE 5.1   Key Elements of Personal Journals

feedback and a chance to showcase their work. Further, after our small-group sessions, I often gather the journals of the children with whom I have worked that morning, and show the journal entries in the subsequent whole-class meeting. This whole-class setting allows us to revisit our read-aloud books once again if children have drawn and/or dictated about any of the day's read-aloud books, and for me to highlight certain aspects of text, meaning, and visuals from the read-aloud books, or aspects that I had missed and the children themselves discovered and featured in their journals. During this time, which lasts about five to seven minutes, I also point out specific aspects of children's increasing skill in drawing, representation, and language. I further use this occasion to highlight specific literacy similarities and connections across children's journals, and to emphasize any role that peer collaboration and support played in the children's drawing and dictation.

For educators, then, personal journals are compact and portable for teaching and assessment, provide an ongoing record of children's literacy engagement and development for noticing shifts and patterns in children's book interests and literacy learning, and provide ample documentation data for inquiry and reflection on our instructional strategies and children's growth.

For families, the personal journals provide evidence of a classroom literacy process that is both developmentally appropriate and intellectually challenging, a portfolio of children's connections to favorite books and stories, a visual representation of their children's literacy interests and knowledge, and a chronological record for families to share in their children's evolving talents for dictation and art over several months and even years.

Drawing

There are several strategies that I use for supporting children's drawing in their personal journals such as creating opportunities for children to represent their funds of knowledge, their favorite books, attention to engaging visuals from the read-alouds, and using drawing as a springboard for dictation (Figure 5.2).

Representation of Funds of Knowledge

I encourage children to represent key aspects of their school, home, neighborhood, and community lives. Their journals are an important blank canvas on which to depict the people, objects, experiences, ideas, and feelings that matter to the children and that might not find suitable expression and representation in other areas of the preschool literacy curriculum, but that contribute to the social, cultural, and intellectual fabric of the classroom community. These kinds of open-ended opportunities to draw their families, where they live, their favorite pursuits and hobbies, their friends, and their most treasured experiences bring out children's talents, interests, and experiences onto the drawn page.

Children often discuss what they are drawing, relying on their funds of knowledge through out-of-school experiences that in turn connect children socially in the classroom. For example, I sat with Tyrone, Alonso, and Maile as they drew in their journals.

TYRONE: (speaking to our small group) I'm drawing my haircut.
ALONSO: My mom cut my hair. (He shows me his hair.)

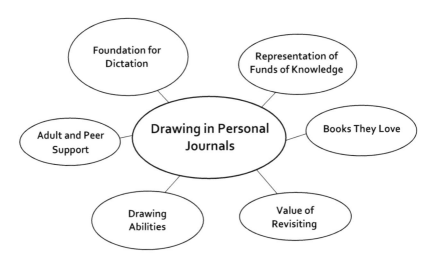

FIGURE 5.2   Drawing in Personal Journals

MAILE: My mom cut my hair. (She shows me her hair, too.) And I want to keep it long like Rapunzel.

One child's drawing spontaneously leads to home-based experiences (family hair-cuts) and a literary allusion (Rapunzel), and this process reveals the "synergy, a unique reciprocity" (Gregory, 2001, p. 309) underlying the children's individual drawing talents and shared social engagement.

For those children who may prefer not to speak up during whole-class read-alouds and/or small-group literacy formats, drawing also provides an avenue for self-expression and sharing of ideas and experiences that does not require oral language and interaction with others. In essence, children's representation of their ideas and feelings and experiences on the drawn page gives voices to their lives, and strengthens their individual, social, and artistic presence within the classroom literary community. Sooner or later, one of the children sitting nearby will notice a more "quiet" child's drawing and remark on it, prompting the interest and engagement of other children, who might start drawing something similar or ask the child a question or make a comment.

Books They Love

I also encourage children to consider drawing aspects of the whole-class read-aloud books that they enjoy and find meaningful. During the read-aloud session, I front-load this idea by suggesting to the children that they might be interested in drawing a particular visual from a read-aloud book in the upcoming small group work. Then, when I gather with a small group of children, I extend my sugges-tions to specific children ("Ankur, you really seemed to enjoy this book when we just read it on the rug, do you want to look at it and see if there's something you want to draw from the book?") or I simply place a few of the books that I know the children have enjoyed on the table and let them choose a book to look at as the basis or inspiration for their drawing.

Value of Revisiting

> ### KEY IDEA
>
> Revisiting read-aloud books for the purpose of drawing in personal journals encourages children to revisit favorite characters, scenes, visu-als, and plot points, and to do so within the collaborative, social nature of a small group.

Sitting at a table with their open personal journal and the chance to choose any of the books from the day's read-aloud, as well as other books from recent read-aloud sessions that I keep in my bookbag, children have the opportunity to choose from about a dozen familiar books from three or four weeks' worth of read-alouds and book browsing. These regular opportunities support children in revisiting and recalling essential aspects of plot, character, language, content, message, visuals, and author's style within and across an evolving repertoire of books.

The regular routine of revisiting also encourages children to strengthen their drawing skills and to deepen their aesthetic appreciation of a book's visuals and format by either using the book as a direct model to draw from, or scanning the book and then drawing from that immediate memory. I have also worked with children who do not bother looking at a book again after the whole-class read-aloud, and instead proceed to draw from memory a specific scene, object, or character from a book. If children are interested in a specific page, for instance a double-page spread from Jerry Pinkney's *The Lion & the Mouse*, I use a sturdy metal clip or two to pin back the pages so a child can freely draw while looking at the open pages. The opening up of a book in this fashion also sends an open invitation to other nearby children to look at the page, and to consider also drawing something from or about the open page. The open page also invites peer collaboration and dialogue about the visuals, and gives children a common focal point for an exchange of ideas for drawing and dictation. The use of the digital stories and books can be used in the same fashion, as a specific page can be left open on a computer or tablet for children to observe, discuss, and draw.

The opportunity for children to look back over previous entries in their journals also serves as built-in support to jog their memory, and I ask children when they first come to the small-group table, "Do you want to add to one of your pages, or do you want to start something new?" If I know that a child has been drawing and dictating a series of entries on a particular author or a particular book, or has shown a continuing interest in a certain topic from school or home, then I will look at a certain page or two with children to see if they want to continue the content of their drawings. There are other children, though, who rarely like to revisit and add to their previous journal pages and enjoy drawing and dictating new content each time.

Drawing Abilities – Adult and Peer Support

How much do children's artistic inclinations and fine-motor skills influence their level of engagement and investment in their drawing? I find that most young children eagerly draw and are almost immediately invested in their personal journals no matter their drawing and fine-motor skills, and they are rarely concerned that what they have drawn actually looks like a person or specific object in a conventional sense. Children usually understand at some deep level that drawing is a developmental process, and as long as they feel that they are representing something of personal and social value and import, they are pleased with their current levels of drawing and representational ability. This process is also a powerful medium for new language learners and emergent bilinguals, allowing them a non-linguistic pathway to social and artistic acceptance and inclusion in the group.

There are times though when I directly support children's drawing in their personal journals. There are certain children who benefit from extra support and encouragement to draw, and occasionally need an initial boost and guidance so that they see and feel both that they have something to draw and that they have the basic motor and artistic knowledge to draw something and feel socially included in the peer group. For these children, I often enlist another child to help draw part of an object (a rock or a house) or an animal (such as a ladybug) as a form of peer-scaffolding, or I ask another child to show the child how to draw a house or animal on another piece of paper. Sometimes, children's drawings for their peers bear little resemblance to a "house" or "ladybug," but I find that it is the social intention and goodwill behind the drawing that pleases all of the children involved.

For example, Michael wanted to draw the bear from *Bear and Hare: Snow!* (Gravett, 2015), which I had just read to a small group of children. Michael spontaneously asked Natasha, sitting beside him, to draw the bear. Natasha stood up and walked to another table, then came back with a small stencil of a bear made of a hard, red, cardboard-like material. I had no idea that the stencil existed in the classroom, nor would I have thought of using a stencil. In a moment of developmental, social, and artistic responsiveness and peer support, Natasha handed the stencil to Michael and suggested he use it to draw the bear. Michael said, "Natasha, the bear is brown." So Natasha helped him select a brown marker, and watched intently as Michael started to trace the outline of the bear from the stencil, and then carefully color in the bear with the thin brown marker. When he finished drawing, he brought me his journal for dictation, and given his success with the bear, I suggested that Michael draw the scarf around the bear's neck in the illustration. Michael sat back down and then asked, "Mr. Meier, do you have any white? I want to draw the snow." (In the book, Bear is wearing a scarf outside in the snow.) I told him that the snow would be hard to draw as it would be white on white, and I suggested he draw the red scarf instead, which he happily did.

There are other occasions, which are rare, when I help a child form a line or shape by placing my hand over the child's hand to make the motion, or I draw a shape on another piece of paper. I do believe that experiences with observational drawing from nature and science-related projects help children's drawing knowledge and skill, and that there can be an important transfer from observational drawing to the more open-ended format of drawing in personal journals. When children feel that their drawing attempts are accepted by adults and by peers, they are almost always motivated to draw more and to take more risks. By and large, though, preschool children are undaunted by the challenge of trying to draw something even from a page of such exquisite artists as Jerry Pinkney, Grace Lin, and Allen Say.

Drawing as a Foundation for Dictation

Whether children draw a recognizable object or human figure, or lines and curves that are not recognizable in a conventional sense, both forms of symbolic representation carry meaning and personal import for young children of Color. In essence, the marks "speak" to children and they are fertile ground for supporting children's dictation. Just as Dale Long (Chapter 3) commented that when children first learn a letter in their name, they "own" that letter, so too do young children delight in "owning" the symbols they use in their drawings.

Sometimes a single character in a book captures a child's interest in drawing. On the computer, we read the digital book *Singing in the Rain* (Kumar & Chaudhry, 2015), which tells the story of a singer who meets a music-loving dinosaur. Brian was so taken with the appearance of a dinosaur in this digital story that he called it the "dinosaur story," and he wanted to draw something about the dinosaur. It was Brian's very first time working in his personal journal, and so I helped him ease into the activity. I advanced the pages of the story on my computer until we came to a visual showing a stegosaurus, and Brian wanted to stop there. Since the story only advances by clicking the trackpad, the digital book stayed open to the page as Brian worked in his journal. He said he didn't know what to draw and so I suggested he draw the eyes, which he did with two large, black circles and pupils inside. He wanted to draw the scales next, but was unsure how, so I held his hand while he held the marker, and I slowly guided the marker as I said, "Up, down, up, down, makes the scales." Brian was pleased and drew some on his own.

Brian wanted to draw "the body" of the dinosaur next, and so I enlisted a nearby child, Maile, to help Brian, and Maile drew a large body-like circle for Brian. Brian then wanted to draw the man pictured beside the dinosaur on the page in the book, and so I again held his hand and gently guided him to draw a simple human figure. "He needs a stick. I need a stick," Brian said, looking at the human figure in the book holding up a tall wooden stick. He drew the stick on this own.

I then asked, "Are you ready to do your dictation now?" Brian said, "What's dictation?" I said, "It's when you say something about your drawing or anything you want, and I write it down." Brian eagerly dictated, "The stegosaurus had a spike and a mouth and eyes and a person and the rain." I asked if he wanted to dictate anything else. He paused, and so I asked, "Do you want to write, 'I learned to draw it by myself?'" Brian nodded. In the next section, I discuss other strategies for promoting children's meaningful dictation.

Dictation

The process of dictation has a number of direct benefits for young children such as exploring the building blocks of narrative, oral and written language connections, extending plot points and visuals, literary patterns, knowledge of certain literacy conventions, and a sense of aesthetics (Figure 5.3).

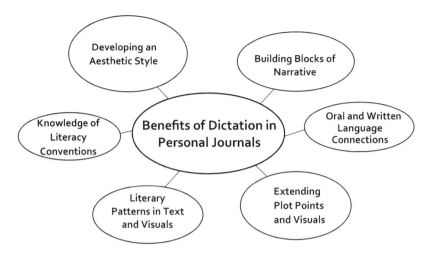

FIGURE 5.3   Key Elements of Dictation in Personal Journals

Building Blocks of Narrative

The structure of a whole-class read-aloud followed immediately by a small-group format for book sharing and personal journals offers children the opportunity to dictate language and content that directly links story worlds with the small, personal literacy space of their journals. In their personal journals, children can dictate brief stories, scenes, small moments, observations, and labels that link back to the read-aloud books. This allows children extended practice and experimentation via dictation with the building blocks of narrative development, and the telling of small and meaningful anecdotes and stories. Children can tell a story or relate an experience both in their journal and off the page, in conversation with peers and adults. This format supports children's interests in and knowledge of story worlds both from the read-aloud books and their own personal, family, and community narratives. It is a regular opportunity for children to build upon their narrative-related funds of knowledge and to particularize their knowledge within the local, socially and culturally relevant format of the small-group dictation work and collaboration.

Oral Language and Written Language Connections

KEY IDEA

Linking dictation with high-quality, culturally and child responsive children's books and children's drawings promotes a rich tapestry

> of children's oral and written language, and speaks to their desire to become conversational partners, artists, and authors.

The process of dictation enables children to see how their oral language can be adapted to written language on the page of their personal journals. This is often not a direct transfer, though, as there is a transformation from thought to speech to written language (Vygotsky, 1978). How we frame the dictation activity, then, influences children's thinking and oral language as they link their drawing, their ideas and feelings, and the specific vocabulary and syntax and style of their dictation.

Given the complexity of linking the drawn symbols, thought, and oral language, it is important to provide children with a range of open-ended and more direct prompts to successfully participate in the dictation process:

- "What's going on here?" (in a child's drawing)
- "Please tell me about your drawing. It looks like a new kind of drawing for you."
- "What is this?" (as I point to a drawn object or figure)
- "Let's do your dictation together. What story would you like to tell?"
- "Do you also want to dictate something about the park like Maria just did? I heard you both discussing the park."
- "Do you want to dictate something from this book or that book?" (as I point to the books that the child had open on the table)
- "Do you want to add something from the dictation that you did last week? I remember you enjoyed dictating about your new baby brother."

I intentionally choose certain prompts for specific children to support their developmental trajectory or history in terms of drawing and dictation. I also select prompts that support their drawing and read-aloud interests from what just transpired during our whole-class read-aloud.

I especially tend to use more specific language prompts with certain children who might need support for the individual language needs:

1. Younger preschoolers who are at the early stages of strengthening their oral language abilities and understanding the dictation process
2. New language learners who are learning new English word meanings, the sense of words in context, and syntactical structures
3. Children with special needs who might need extra assistance with speech articulation, vocabulary comprehension, and oral language production

For these children, I use a range of strategies to support their dictation that directly link to our read-aloud books as well as other children's drawing and dictation. Both of these resources provide a model for the children in terms of ideas, content, artistic representation, and specific language. First, I often refer to specific places in our familiar read-aloud books that they might want to draw and then dictate about. When we revisit these books, I try to select books that I know the children are most interested in and that do not offer overly challenging vocabulary, syntax, or literary language.

For example, I worked with Mariah, whose receptive English was more proficient than her English production, to look closely at Brian Wildsmith's (1986) *What a Tale*, a patterned language book that works well with new language learners. Mariah had looked at it for her drawing, carefully drawing different tails of the animals in the book.

Reflective Teaching Journal – December 5

"Do you want to look at the book again that you used for your drawing, and use it for your dictation?" Mariah nodded. I pointed to each tail pictured in the book and I waited so that Mariah and I would both say "tail" together at the end of each sentence – "This is the spotted ____ (tail). This is the striped big ___ (tail). That's the bushy ____ (tail). The long ____ (tail)." We then looked at Mariah's drawing in her personal journal, and as I repeated the sentence from the book for each animal's tail, Mariah and I again said "tail" together and I wrote down a few of the book's sentences as her dictation.

While I do not regularly provide such extensive scaffolding for children, I do find it occasionally beneficial to provide specific language and literary frames for children to follow and eventually to internalize and use. This is especially effective when used in conjunction with books with patterned text and repeated syntactical structures.

Extending Plot Points and Visuals

As noted earlier, I begin each small-group drawing and dictation activity by either rereading one or two of the whole-group read-alouds, pointing out certain visuals or plot events in a book, and/or placing the read-aloud books on the table in front of the children for their own informal book browsing and reading. These strategies help children extend certain visuals and plot points from the read-aloud books and provide ideas for their drawing and dictation.

For example, I worked with Exavier as he drew and dictated in connection with *Bear and Hare Go Fishing*, which we had just read in our whole-class read-aloud and I had brought to our small group's table.

Reflective Teaching Journal – January 7

Exavier drew lines in blue and red, and dictated, "A bear and a hare go fishing." (Exavier pointed to the extra space on the left of his journal page, and told me that there was space to write there.) I thought of extending his one-sentence dictation of "A bear and hare go fishing," and so I suggested we get the book and look at it, which we did. Exavier said that he liked the page that contained the phrase that he recalled as "big ol' fish." I then expanded the phrase into a sentence and said, "Do you want to dictate, 'At the end, he catches a big ol' fish?'" Exavier agreed and I wrote the second sentence, and then we read the two sentences back.

This last page featured a single engaging plot point and visual of Bear catching the fish that extended Exavier's interest in drawing and dictating about the book.

There are also occasions when I ask children if they want to start their dictation before they've finished drawing in their journal. In these situations, I notice that children are especially interested in a read-aloud book, and that I can help deepen their drawing and dictation as we revisit certain parts of a book together. For example, I worked with Exavier on his dictation as he drew and talked about *Frederick's Fables* (Lionni, 1997).

Reflective Teaching Journal – December 12

Exavier sat next to Lupe, and both looked at *Frederick's Fables* (Lionni, 1997). Exavier drew a long wavy line in thin blue with a small human figure on top. "Frederick is right here," he said to Lupe, turning the pages of the book and pointing to Frederick as Lupe looked on. I asked Exavier if he wanted to start his dictation before he finished his drawing. Looking at what he had drawn so far, Exavier dictated, "This is Frederick," and then stopped. I asked, "What did he collect?" Exavier said, "He got his words," which I wrote as I repeated his sentence out loud. I asked, "And what else? What did he gather from the sky?" Exavier paused, not sure what to say. Then he said, "The sunrays," which I wrote. I asked, "And what else did he collect?" We looked again at *Frederick* and reread part of the text. Exavier said, "Colors," and I wrote it down. I then asked, "Anything else?" Exavier said, "The mice helped him get a better voice," which I then wrote down. Our rereading prompted Exavier to remember that Frederick had cleared his throat toward the end of the story and before he recited his poem.

Literary Patterns in Text and Visuals

KEY IDEA

When we as adults point to engaging plot points and visuals, and link these to literary patterns in books, we extend children's understanding of important concepts about print and what print can do for them as literary users, producers, and collaborators.

The linking of the read-alouds with children's dictation also allows children to extend their understanding of literacy patterns in text and visuals.

For example, Lupe was intrigued with Brian Wildsmith's (1987) *What a Tale*, and used this book as the basis for her drawing and dictation. More proficient in English than Mariah, whose dictation I scaffolded in an earlier example in this section, Lupe used her considerable language skills to self-scaffold her dictation.

Reflective Teaching Journal – January 7

As Lupe held the marker to the side in her fingers, she drew a face on the cover of her journal and wrote her name. She then very carefully drew in brown marker the tails from Brian Wildsmith's (1986) *What a Tale*, and readily dictated from left to right, "This is the spotted tail. This is the striped big tail. That's the bushy tail. The long tail." I then asked her which tail belongs to each animal, and without looking at the book, which was under another book the entire time, Lupe recited her dictation in correct order again, "Dog, cat, fox, monkey."

The patterning of image and language from the book provided Lupe with a template for re-patterning the images of the animals' tails along with their verbal labels in her dictation.

Knowledge of Literacy Conventions

KEY IDEA

Drawing and dictation in personal journals strengthens preschool children's emerging alphabetic and sound-symbol knowledge when we can pinpoint small moments that integrate certain aspects of content and literacy mechanics.

Although it is challenging to integrate specific literacy knowledge while retaining the playful and child-centered nature of drawing and dictation in the personal journals, there are a few ways to achieve this integration.

For example, this integration makes developmental sense for those children who are interested and capable of copying actual conventional text from a book. For instance, Tiara wanted to copy a sentence from *Bear & Hare: Snow!* (Gravett, 2015) in her journal.

Reflective Teaching Journal – March 24

In her personal journal, Tiara drew snowballs from *Bear & Hare: Snow!* (Gravett, 2015) in purple, and then tried to copy a sentence from the book. She needed more room on her journal page, but she managed to copy half of it. Tiara then drew a few more figures and objects, and her ensuing dictation was about her friends in the room, which continued a theme of friendship that she had put in her earlier dictations.

Tiara's self-initiated copying showcased her interest in trying to write conventional text and her ability to form the letters, and gave her practice writing conventional letters and words and in left-to-right directionality and spacing her writing on the page. While most of the children that I have worked with are more interested in drawing and some scribbling of words or writing of random or patterned strings of letters, a few children are eager to try their hand at writing and copying text from a book as a developmentally supportive first step.

During a small-group session, Alonso drew a few objects and then wrote the patterned string of "AABBCC" with a line underneath, and then another row of "AABBCC" with another line underneath, and he dictated, "I did my writing." He drew the same pattern on the next page. For the first page, he dictated, "I did my writing," and for the second page, he dictated, "More letters." On the next page, he drew a few yellow shapes and then dictated, "It's fire."

On this day, I noticed several picture cards on the board in the front of the classroom that started with the letter "V/v" as the class had recently started studying a different letter every week or so. Given Alonso's interest in writing letters, I wondered how we might incorporate the letters in Alonso's dictation, and so I suggested to Alonso that we put in some "v" words. I thought of adding, "It's very, very hot," and he agreed. Then he dictated, "I'll let the fire burn."

The following week, he drew one large shape and then dictated, "This is a big moustache! It is scratchy and itchy." By this point, the class had moved on to the letter "M/m," and there were new visuals on the board of objects that started with "m" and a poster showing the words to the Miss Mary Mack rhyme. I pointed to poster and told Alonso that his dictated word "moustache" started with "M/m," the letter they were learning.

A few weeks later the class had moved on to identifying the letter "S/s," and in our small group we happened to read a digital book about a ballerina and another about a snake. As I passed out the personal journals, I suggested that the children might want to draw something from the snake book, which I thought was easier to draw than human figures from the ballet book. Serena, though, proceeded to draw a human figure to the right of the page, a sun in the upper-left corner, and three large "S" letters in yellow in the middle of the page. She then dictated, "The snake has a tutu and it really likes to dance. The snake wants to dance with me, and I'm a ballerina. The sun is bright." I pointed to the poster at the front of the room and told Serena that her dictated words "sun" and "snake" and the three letter "Ss" that she had written all contained the letter "S/s" that they were learning.

Developing an Aesthetic Style

Drawing and dictation also help children develop their own individual style and sense of aesthetics in their journals. For instance, on one occasion Carlos was quite motivated and engaged with orchestrating several varied linguistic, visual, and aesthetic elements of his drawing and dictation.

Reflective Teaching Journal – December 17

Carlos wrote his name and a human figure on the front of his journal. He then wanted to write "Ramirez," his last name, and since he did not know how to write the letters, I wrote it for him in small letters, which Carlos then copied in marker next to "Carlos." He then drew a new intricate drawing, in his usual careful and methodological style, all in thin black marker. He then dictated, "This is a big tower," and stopped, not wanting to dictate any more. I then suggested more possibilities for text – "Rooms in his tower?" "A tall tower?" He then restarted his dictation as he pointed to qualities of color and background in his drawing, "Black works on white, and white works on black." He then added, "It has lots of little rooms and one big one for a dinosaur. It's for a T-Rex."

Carlos experimented with integrating drawing (a human figure and the tower), written language (writing his first name and copying his last name), oral language to written language connections (dictation – "This is a big tower"), and insights on color and light in his drawing ("Black works on white, and white works on black"). Carlos's orchestration of all of these elements helped promote an evolving sense of personal and individual aesthetics for Carlos.

Personal journals also allow children to pursue their own particular sense of aesthetics over a long period of time. The journals promote ample developmental time and artistic space to tinker, experiment, and focus on specifics aspects of color, line, shadow, movement, texture, and emotion in both drawing and dictation. For example, during every small-group session, Koah loved to spend 30 to 45 minutes continually drawing in his journal. He loved to use thin makers, carefully using the marker first to trace the outline of his drawings and then using other markers to draw over the tracing marks (Figures 5.4 and 5.5). His careful drawings and use of tracing served as an intricate aesthetic foundation for his dictation, and a self-scaffolded skill that he returned to and extended each week.

Koah also liked to explore one color, seeing its effect both as an arresting visual in itself and also to accentuate and complement his dictated text (Figure 5.6). In the original drawing, the fire is a bright swirling red and his "construction" scaffolding below and to the right of the fire is also depicted in red. He only used black for the fire pit base below the fire and for indicating the ground at the bottom of the drawing. The extensive use of the color red as juxtaposed with a bit of black created a striking visual.

On other occasions, Koah played with several colors on the same page, as well as drawing a range of different objects (Figure 5.7). He used all the color of the rainbow for the rainbow at the top of his drawing, and red, blue, black, and purple for the other objects on the page.

Koah also liked to play with the movement of his drawn lines, creating movement and motion via three-dimensional constructions and mechanical contraptions on the two-dimensional journal page (Figure 5.8).

Over the course of the year, Koah created an ongoing artistic series of his carefully traced and designed drawings, complemented by his succinct dictated

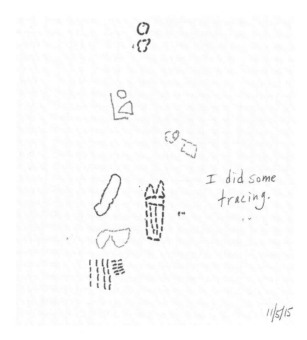

FIGURE 5.4 Koah: "I Did Some Tracing."

This is
the sun.

And I
did
some
more
tracing.

flower

light
castles

the 5
page

a
flower

my house

11/12/15

FIGURE 5.5 Koah: "And I Did Some More Tracing."

We're putting on a fire pit and burning wood.

This puts fire on.

This is my construction.

Koah
10/29/15

FIGURE 5.6 Koah: "We're Putting on a Fire Pit and Burning Wood."

descriptions, which functioned in a way like titles for his art. The year-long opportunity to draw with frequency, to be afforded ample time to draw, to revisit his previous drawings, and to complement his drawing with dictated oral language provided Koah with an ongoing forum for honing his drawing skills and aesthetic sensibilities.

This is a rainbow.

11/5/15

KOAH

And I did a cylinder.

And I drew my house.

We had some flowers.

And 2 coconut trees.

FIGURE 5.7 Koah: "This Is a Rainbow."

Sharing

After our small-group work with the read-aloud books and the personal journals, we reconvene as a whole class, and I share the drawing and dictation of those children with whom I have worked on that particular day. In general, I show each

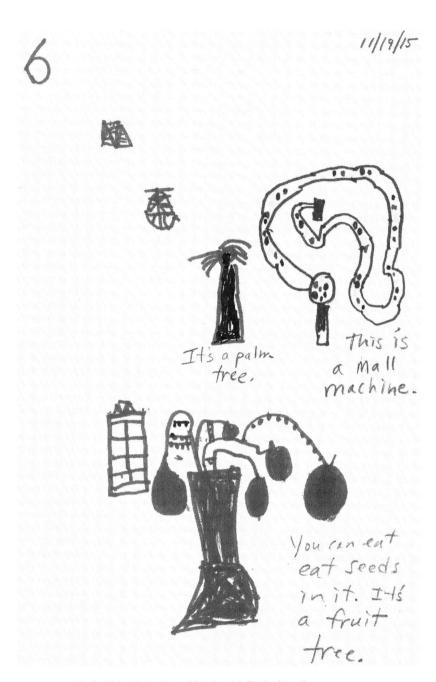

FIGURE 5.8   Koah: "It's a Palm Tree. This Is a Mall Machine."

child's drawings and read their dictation, and I highlight certain aspects of the children's journal using several strategies:

- Call attention to a child's achievements in terms of aesthetics ("Let's look carefully at how Koah used tracing lines to help with his drawing.")
- Explain the process of a child's drawing ("Maile started by drawing around the edge of the page to make an outline of her house, and then she started to draw the inside and all of these parts that you see here.")
- Highlight the socially collaborative and supportive nature of children's drawing in the small-group format ("Michael really wanted to draw Bear from *Bear & Hare* and so Natasha helped him. She got a bear stencil and brought it to Michael, who used it to draw Bear, and here is the drawing.")
- Show the connections across the children's journals to show how content can be linked and supported by peers ("Alicia's dictation talks about a donut! How do you think she had the idea to draw and dictate about a donut?!" I then read another child's journal in which the child had been the first in the small group to draw and dictate about a donut.)
- Highlight children's special drawing and dictation talents and skills ("So if you want to learn how to draw a really great ladybug, just ask Serena." "If you want to draw an Anansi spider, talk to Adelia." "If you want to draw a monster truck with a number 4 on it, ask Khalil to help you.")
- Conduct the child's dictation on the spot (On occasion children in our small group finish their drawings, but we run out of time for their dictation. So I ask the children to stand with me in front of the class and dictate text to accompany their drawing. It's helpful modeling for the whole class to see the process.)

These sharing strategies extend the children's engagement with their individual journals, and deepen the communal classroom effort in linking drawing and dictation. The sharing also completes the circle of our literacy work and play, in that we start with a whole-class read-aloud of three to four books, then revisit those books and others in a small group, then engage in drawing and discussion in the small group, and then finally share specific aspects of the children's journals with the whole class.

Chapter Summary and Reflections

In this chapter, I provided a range of organizational structures and practical strategies to strengthen children's drawing and dictation in their personal journals. The journal process is best carried out within a small-group format, which provides ample time and teaching space for adults to guide and support children's literacy learning and social engagement. The small-group format allows for opportunities to revisit favorite books from the whole-class read-alouds, and for unhurried and communal book browsing and discussion, as well as the integration of the books in the children's drawing and dictation.

The format also provides a predictable routine for young children to engage with and support each other's ideas and skills for drawing and dictation. This provides a responsive public forum and performative space for children of Color to showcase their individual and collective literary and aesthetics talents, interests, and skills. The whole-class gathering after the dictation and drawing activities is a communal sharing and celebration of the children's achievements. It helps make visible children's individual literacy skills and talents, the social and academic ways that children have supported each other's drawing and dictation, and direct connections to children's funds of knowledge (Campano, Ghiso, & Welch, 2016; González, Moll, & Amanti, 2006; Moll, Amanti, Neff, & Gonzalez, 1992) from their homes and communities as well as emerging school-based knowledge of high-quality, responsive children's books (Yenika-Agbaw & Napoli, 2011).

When preschool children are provided with open-ended literacy activities founded upon the acquisition of specific literacy knowledge, they gain increasing flexibility with oral and written language texts (Dyson, 2016; Gregory, 2008). Through this evolving process, children gain an inner sense of control and knowledge of the internal workings of texts as well as an outer, social exhibition of this increasing mastery and achievement. Within the public, communal forum of the classroom and school, it is important that children of Color showcase their increasing flexibility in manipulating texts and integrating symbol systems in their reading, drawing, dictation, and early writing. This process builds layers of kinship within the classroom for children of Color, and does so within the social, intellectual, and aesthetic context of shared literacy engagement and development and aesthetically pleasing and meaningful literacy products. It is important, too, that their literary products are produced with peers and adults, and shared and made public within the classroom community as literary products that matter and are valued (Delpit, 2008).

In the next chapter, I discuss how the professional growth process of inquiry and reflection can help us see the value of the literacy structures and strategies presented in this chapter. The next chapter particularly highlights our own roles as adult learners committed to learning and growing in terms of our literacy knowledge and instruction over the trajectory of our careers.

END-OF-CHAPTER REFLECTIONS

- How do the drawing and dictation strategies described in this chapter showcase the literacy talents of children of Color?
- What do you now see as the potential of using personal journals to promote a literacy community in a preschool classroom?

- Which ideas and strategies for using personal journals in a small-group format might you add or adapt from this chapter for your teaching?
- Which ideas and strategies for promoting children's drawing and dictation might you add or adapt from this chapter?
- Can you think of an individual child or group of children who would benefit in specific ways from implementing some of the chapter's ideas and strategies?

References

Campano, G., Ghiso, M. P., & Welch, B. J. (2016). *Partnering with immigrant communities: Action through literacy.* New York, NY: Teachers College Press.

Delpit, L. (2008). No kinda sense. In L. Delpit & J. K. Dowdy (Eds.), *The skin that we speak: Thoughts on language and culture in the classroom* (pp. 31–48). New York, NY: The New Press.

Dyson, A. H. (Ed.). (2016). *Child cultures, schooling, and literacy: Global perspectives on composing unique lives.* New York, NY: Routledge.

González, N., Moll, L. C., & Amanti, C. (Eds.). (2006). *Funds of knowledge: Theorizing practices in households, communities, and classrooms.* New York, NY: Routledge.

Gravett, E. (2015). *Bear & hare: Snow!* New York, NY: Simon & Schuster Books for Young Readers.

Gregory, E. (2001). Sisters and brothers as language and literacy teachers: Synergy between siblings playing and working together. *Journal of Early Childhood Literacy, 1*(3), 301–322.

Gregory, E. (2008). *Learning to read in a new language: Making sense of words and worlds* (2nd ed.). Los Angeles, CA: Sage.

Kumar, M., & Chaudhry, M. (2015). *Singing in the rain.* Bengaluru: Pratham Books.

Lionni, L. (1997). *Frederick's fables: A treasury of 16 Leo Lionni favorites.* New York, NY: Knopf Books for Young Readers.

Moll, L. C., Amanti, C., Neff, D., & Gonzalez, N. (1992). Funds of knowledge for teaching: Using a qualitative approach to connect homes and classrooms. *Theory Into Practice, 31*(2), 132–141.

Vasquez, V. M. (2017). Critical literacy. *Oxford Research Encyclopedia of Education.* doi:10.1093/acrefore/9780190264093.013.20

Vygotsky, L. S. (1978). *Mind in society.* Cambridge, MA: Harvard University Press.

Wildsmith, B. (1987). *What a tale.* Oxford: Oxford University Press.

Yenika-Agbaw, V., & Napoli, M. (2011). *African and African American children's and adolescent literature in the classroom: A critical guide: Black studies and critical thinking* (Vol. 11). New York, NY: Peter Lang.

SECTION III
Increased Visibility

6

TEACHER INQUIRY, DOCUMENTATION, AND REFLECTION – A PROFESSIONAL PROCESS FOR TRANSFORMING LITERACY EDUCATION

OPENING REFLECTIONS

- What do you know about the process of teacher inquiry, documentation, and reflection?
- If you are learning about this process in your initial preservice education, what are the most appealing elements of this process?
- If you learned about the inquiry process in your inservice professional development, what are a few key ways that you've applied elements of the inquiry to your literacy teaching?
- If you are interested in forming or joining an inquiry group at your site or with other colleagues elsewhere, what would you like to learn from the inquiry group process for supporting the literacy talents of young children of Color?

In this chapter, I focus on how teacher inquiry, documentation, and reflection can deepen our understanding of children's literacy talents and strengthen our teaching practices. In Chapter 1, I discussed certain foundational ideas undergirding teacher inquiry, documentation, and reflection. Here in this chapter, I examine in more depth several key elements, and I provide examples of how these elements come together to deepen our literacy knowledge and expertise.

> **KEY IDEA**
>
> Inquiry, documentation, and reflection form the foundation for nurturing our minds and hearts as observant, dedicated, and reflective practitioners and teachers of literacy. This process becomes deepened through the formation of regular, structured inquiry groups where educators present, share, and dialogue about their data collection and analysis regarding strengthening the literacy learning of young children of Color.

Teacher Inquiry, Documentation, and Reflection – Key Elements for Raising Our Awareness and Knowledge of the Literacy Talents of Children of Color

> If I believe that all children are bright and resourceful and talented, I need to highlight that for myself, my children and my families.
> —*Isauro Michael Escamilla, Preschool Teachers*

The overall goal of using inquiry, documentation, and reflection is to uncover hidden aspects of our literacy teaching and children's literacy learning, and to use this data for conceptualizing, teaching, and monitoring a strength-based approach to literacy education. In this journey, it is important that we take an active stance of ownership and agency toward our inquiry and see ourselves as conducting systematic, impassioned inquiry on essential aspects of our literacy instruction and the literacy talents and resources of children of Color and their families.

The inquiry cycle or process includes several components or steps – observation, data collection, documentation, narrative, self-reflection and reflection with colleagues, and instructional change (Figure 6.1).

Observation

In the initial stage of the process, we first focus on what we want to observe and collect data on. There are a number of aspects of children's literacy learning that we can collect data on, and these elements often involve examining the "what" of children's literacy engagement and learning:

- What books do children most enjoy sharing and discussing with each other?
- What are children talking about when they discuss books?
- What languages do children draw upon in these discussions?
- What kinds of stories do children like to tell?

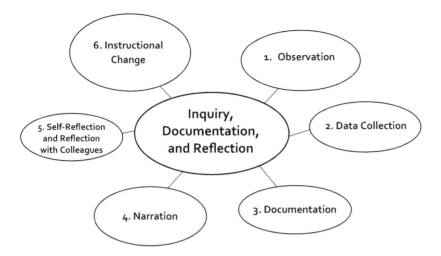

FIGURE 6.1   Key Inquiry Elements

- What kinds of artwork do children enjoy creating?
- What do children like to dictate?
- What kinds of texts are children able to copy in their early writing?
- What do children know about the alphabet and other scripts?

A second step involves looking at the processes and the "how" that undergird our literacy teaching:

- How to structure effective whole-class and small-group literacy activities?
- How to make deeper connections between children's artwork and dictation?
- How to find new criteria for selecting child responsive and culturally responsive children's books?
- How to identify the literacy needs of the multilingual children in my classroom?
- How to confront my biases around my views of certain children's literacy abilities?
- How to create new home-school literacy connections?

At a later stage, we can focus on children's learning and our teaching in an integrated fashion – watching, listening, and feeling for key connections (and missed connections) between our literacy teaching and the children's engagement and learning. In these instances, the early inquiry steps of the "what" and the "how" turn into the "why:"

- Why are culturally responsive books so valuable for children of Color?

- Why do certain children rely on each other for ideas in their drawing, while others prefer to draw on their own?
- Why is it beneficial for us to link word meaning and word sense in our literacy teaching?
- Why is it valuable to mix whole-group and small-group literacy routines and activities?
- Why is dictation a helpful process for children to learn certain concepts of print?
- Why does a certain child do so well in small-group literacy activities but has a more challenging time in whole-group activities?

KEY IDEA

Powerful inquiry, documentation, and reflection ultimately connects the "what," the "how," and the "why" of teaching and learning in the classrooms and educational contexts for young children of Color. This integrated connection empowers educators as thoughtful, sentient beings curious and knowledgeable about strengthening the literacy learning of children of Color.

As we integrate the "what" and the "how" and the "why" in our inquiry, it is important to remember that inquiry is an ongoing, often humbling, process of professional growth and discovery. As preschool teacher Sarah Overton notes, "I found it valuable that we become excited in our inquiry when we're wrong, when we don't find out exactly what we are seeking, and we can then ask new questions, just as we want children to do in their own inquiry-based learning."

Data Collection

Data collection refers to the tools that we use in our observations, and it's helpful to use a variety of data collection tools in varied literacy contexts. While there is also some crossover between varied data collection tools, each data collection tool has its particular strengths and benefits:

- Reflective notebooks and journals are effective for jotting down observations, insights, reflections.
- Photographs capture a small moment or a series of steps in a child's learning.
- Audiotaping documents the subtle details of children's oral language and dialogue.
- Videotaping documents nonverbal communication, actions, and behaviors.

- Recording data on chart paper or via other paper-based materials provides a record of children's comments or brainstorm ideas.
- Informally interviewing individual children and families documents their literacy expectations and perspectives.
- Surveys and questionnaires for families gather responses and thoughts on families' literacy goals and practices.
- The regular collection of children's work and play samples provides a chronological history of children's literacy growth over time.
- Informal assessment tools such as portfolios and learning stories provide narrative-based forms of documenting children's learning.

These data collection tools can be mixed and matched over time, and as we gain experience linking data collection tools with what we are observing, we increase our expertise in choosing the most effective tools for specific documentation and reflection purposes. For example, if we are collecting data on children's drawing and dictation as I have done for this book, we can audiotape child and adult oral language, take written notes to remember any nonverbal language and behaviors, take photographs to capture a moment or series of moments in children's literacy learning, and create learning stories that provide a narrative account of children's literacy discoveries and talents.

A word here on the use of electronic devices for data collection. Depending on your professional context and confidentiality expectations, you may use a cell phone, iPad, or other electronic means to videotape children's literacy behaviors, interactions, and processes. There are several advantages to collecting data via video:

- Even a brief video clip of 1-2 minutes can capture an important literacy scene or set of behaviors
- Data can be easily stored and dated chronologically
- Data can be shared with colleagues or families either in person or electronically
- Data can be reviewed multiple times and certain smaller segments can be examined more closely
- Single images can be freeze-framed to create a photograph
- Children enjoy watching and commenting on their literacy work and play via video

I often find it most beneficial to combine and integrate paper or hard copy data collection with electronic data collection. In this process, there is enough freedom for individuals, teaching teams, and an entire early childhood site to select the most useful and beneficial tools, and often, their choices often complement each other, resulting in a more effective and comprehensive data collection effort. For example, over the course of several months or a year, we can take handwritten notes of children's literacy play and work in a teacher reflective journal, photographs of a child's stages of making a drawing captured via an iPad, children's book-browsing conversation and interactions captured via video on an iPad, a collection of hardcopies of a child's early scribbles and writing placed in the child's portfolio folder, and a learning story written to a child with responses by the child's family and also the child.

Reflective Teacher Journals

Teacher inquirers often view a reflective teacher journal or notebook as the single most powerful tool, and the easiest to use, for data collection.

KEY IDEA

Journals provide an easily accessible data collection tool for collecting and preserving a wide range of literacy-related behaviors, talk, and products. If you are unsure about which data collection tool to try first, try a journal and experiment with how you record your observations and reflections.

There are several advantages to using a reflective teaching journal:

- It is portable and easily carried around the learning environment and easily accessible.
- We can quickly jot down a note or observation while we are working with children.
- We can jot down observations on data ranging from a snippet of children's conversation about a book to the content of their dictation.
- It can also function as a teaching tool such as when children want to tell us a story or insight about a book or other literacy material and we write down their thoughts and stories.
- We can date each entry and maintain a chronology of our data collection.
- We can use a journal for more "objective" observations as well as more "subjective" insights and reflections.
- We can create a journal format that suits our style, asking questions for our later reflection, notes to self, or posing possible next steps for instruction.
- If we are not allowed to take photographs of our children, it is possible to draw a child engaged in their literacy learning, or draw a sequence of key events or stages in their learning as a mini-visual or comic book-like sequence.

- We can also use a journal for writing down a stream of consciousness about our thoughts, feelings, and observations about our literacy teaching, and then use this process for taking a deep breath and taking a step back for reflection.
- We can easily paste in a photograph of a child's literacy work or clip an example of their story dictation or early writing.
- A journal is easily shared with a child to show their literacy achievements as well as the child's family for both informal sharing and more formal family conferences.
- A journal is also easily shared with our colleagues informally and in inquiry group meetings.

In Chapters 4 and 5, I relied on excerpts from my own reflective teaching journal to show examples of my literacy teaching and the children's literacy learning and engagement. I took notes on my laptop as I worked with the children in small groups, most often when the children were busily engaged on their own or in conversation with each other, and I also took notes after our literacy session concluded and I had a bit more time and space to recall important details of our literacy work together. In addition to using my computer, I also took handwritten notes on the children's literacy-related behaviors and talk in my journal notebook, which allowed me to jot down snippets of their conversation and dictation that helped jog my memory later when I took more notes in my electronic journal. I also used my handwritten journal notebook to draw what children drew in their own personal journals, which also helped me remember their drawing process and product for later reflection.

Documentation

When we observe and record children's literacy learning and our own teaching through sensitive and thoughtful data collection tools, we engage in the rich and valuable process of documentation. This process refers to the ways that we represent what we consider as important small moments, anecdotes, stories, examples, and products of children's literacy learning, as well as our literacy instruction and the involvement of families in their preschoolers' literacy education. Documentation essentially occurs simultaneously along with our observations and use of data collection tools; it is the systematic way that we collect and represent our most interesting data for later self-reflection and reflection with colleagues. It is also the foundation for what we present and share in teacher inquiry group meetings, and it forms the basis for professional discourse around effective inquiry, documentation, and reflection and important ways to support and strengthen the literacy talents and abilities of children of Color.

KEY IDEA

Documentation comes in a range of forms – from a single photograph of a solo child drawing to a learning story of a small group of children consulting books for information to a documentation panel chronicling a long-term project. The overall goal of all forms of documentation is to pause the teaching-learning process, hold a small moment of learning or a series of learning moments, and reflect on their significance for improving instruction, children's learning, family connections, and the inquiry process itself.

Documentation can take the form of a polished end-product or in-progress or raw documentation (Meier with Chavez, Eung, & Mancina, 2017). There are several effective strategies for keeping and compiling in-progress or raw documentation, which include collecting data on the following:

- Children's literacy products in an informal portfolio
- Photographs of a child's drawing and art, early writing, storytelling, and/or book browsing across a certain period of time
- Personal journals from the small-group format
- Child's literacy engagement in a certain literacy activity or set of activities as captured by audio and/or video

In the next section, I discuss several documentation dimensions that are important to consider for conceptualizing and creating high-quality documentation of children's literacy learning.

Documentation Dimensions

Over the last 20 years, preschool teacher Oscar Chavez, who teaches in the San Francisco Unified School District, has thoughtfully nurtured and tinkered with documentation tools and products in his classroom. Oscar believes that there are several key dimensions for effective documentation, and he and his co-teachers work together to integrate these dimensions to create effective documentation.

KEY DOCUMENTATION DIMENSIONS

- Process and product
- Environmental integration

- Time
- Stages
- Development
- Languages and literacies
- Assessment

The *process and product* dimension refers to documentation as both a process and a set of products, and high-quality documentation often integrates process and product, showing the how and the what of children's literacy learning. *Environmental integration* utilizes different areas of the classroom environment to display documentation processes and products, and is an effective way to show how children's literacy talents can be integrated in all environmental areas.

The *time* dimension involves documentation extended over time to allow ample developmental space for all children's abilities, and most effectively connected with literacy curriculum that affords ample time for children to experiment, discover, discover, and reflect. *Stages* refer to in-process documentation, or "raw documentation," which enables the material to become a "living" example of observation for children, teachers, and families. The *development* dimension refers to the varied forms of documentation, such as "spontaneous" and "initial investigations," and helps us see a developmental continuum of children's engagement and learning and see patterns for children's literacy discoveries and development. *Languages and literacies* involve documentation that integrates children's, teachers', and families' languages and written language scripts in both raw and final documentation. The *assessment* dimension refers to documentation that integrates elements of mandated, summative assessment measures as well other forms of formative assessment such as learning stories and portfolios.

These central dimensions of inquiry and documentation allow Oscar and his co-teachers to tell a story of the evolution of a theme and project. For example, the use of "raw documentation" – such as children's drawings and dictation clipped and displayed horizontally on a pole in the middle of the classroom – provides an ongoing set of investigative and representational evidence and information for the class as a project evolves over time (Figure 6.2).

Oscar and the teachers look at the raw documentation, and ask themselves, "Where can go we this? Or should we stay with this for now? Is it best to involve one child, half the class, or all the children?" The teachers vote with the children about what they want to focus on as the main project, although sometimes there are small projects "on the side" of the classroom's central project. If Oscar's teaching team doesn't extend the raw documentation, the extra material is put away and possibly revisited at a later date.

FIGURE 6.2 Raw Documentation

Narrative

Narrative can take a range of forms and perform a variety of functions in inquiry, documentation, and reflection. High-level, thoughtful inquiry and reflection often rely on the power of story to document, share, and make sense of important literacy teaching and learning. These stories come in many forms – multilingual, signed, verbal, nonverbal, drawn, written, dictated, dramatized, and digital (Sisk-Hilton & Meier, 2016). In placing narrative at the center of the inquiry process, teacher inquirers experience and see the whole of the teaching/learning equation as a set of unfolding stories, "aha" moments, pivotal scenes, and insightful anecdotes. By using narrative to capture and represent children's development, we take on the additional professional role of narrative inquirers, dedicated to using narrative as the primary medium and lens through which to observe, collect information and artifacts, and reflect and share our ideas, findings, and thoughts. We also become more deeply in touch with our teaching imagination and our sense of curiosity as narrative inquiry is "always composed around a particular wonder, a research puzzle" (Clandinin & Connelly, 2000, p. 124).

Narrative also deepens our documentation work as it helps reveal important narrative plot points both for children's learning and for our own teaching, and we can see new ways that these plot points can converge to support the literacy talents and abilities of young children of Color. In this way, narrative and documentation work together like the text and visuals in a high-quality children's picture book, both enhancing the other to tell a well-told story of meaning, value, and import for readers. In the learning story examples that I present later in this chapter, we can see how certain photographs and children's artwork work together to tell a small, well-told documentation story. Again, this functions like a well-told picture book.

Placing story at the heart of the inquiry, documentation, and reflection process also provides pathways for us to reflect on the cultural responsiveness and the equity and social justice ramifications of our literacy teaching. In this way, linking story and inquiry helps us articulate our ever-changing identities as individuals, as members of varied communities, and as professionals. For instance, our personal and professional narratives of learning to read and write when we were young and the stories of our professional growth and development as readers, writers, and teachers are also important for the inquiry and reflection process. When we examine some of our own narratives, and link these narratives to our professional stories of children and their families through learning stories and other means, we bring about new levels of social and educational awareness, agency, and commitment (Goeson, 2014; Stremmel, 2014). For example, in Chapter 3, several of the educators with whom I spoke noted the power of stories, folktales, and songs that their parents and grandparents told and read in varied languages, and how these childhood narratives have influenced their literacy goals and practices for children of Color.

Self-Reflection and Reflection With Inquiry Group Colleagues

The process of linking inquiry, documentation, and reflection with teacher inquiry groups elevates our understanding of strength-based literacy education through professional dialogue and communication with colleagues. In my collaborative work with preschool teachers in inquiry groups, I have witnessed the power of the group for fostering deeper levels of inquiry and reflection. Our participation within an inquiry group, especially over the span of several years, challenges us to improve our self-reflection skills and insights as the group provides reflective mirrors for examining our literacy goals, biases, strategies, and next steps for improving our practice. The communal sharing of our documentation challenges us to sharpen our observational skills with children, tighten our reflective note-taking, improve our video and audio recording, and use photographs to chronicle the small moments of children's learning. As we acquire more data collection tools, and learn to mix and match these tools with more ease and expertise, our documentation becomes more effective and meaningful to individuals in the group as well as the group as a community of literacy inquirers.

There is also something quite powerful in a group setting with colleagues when we sense the confidence and investment in our collective voices and actions when we present our documentation, and when the texts and visuals that we share exhibit a certain degree of truth and authenticity to the literacy talents and abilities of young children of Color as well as our teaching practices. We pay attention in these instances because we sense that a colleague's documentation provides a window onto some discovery or "aha" moment or revelation about a certain child or teaching dilemma. In essence, the collective sharing of our documentation makes children's literacy learning more visible and gives it a new voice, image, and presence.

For instance, over the course of two of our inquiry group meetings, Isauro Michael Escamilla presented two learning stories about Zahid, one of the students in his classroom who pursued a self-initiated project about his family and specifically his dad's immigration journey, which was prompted by Zahid's fascination with the word "*frontera*." As Isauro presented Zahid's learning stories, our entire inquiry group was transfixed by Isauro and his co-teachers' (Alicia Alvarez and Sahara Gonzalez-Garcia) commitment to supporting Zahid's interest beyond the literal meaning of "*frontera*" and instead to explore the concept and significance of what the word meant to Zahid in terms of his family and self-identity. Isauro, Alicia, and Sahara assisted Zahid with researching maps online and in books and then helped reimagine, draw, and paint the border between the U.S. and Mexico, and the route of his father's journey as based upon Zahid's story. We understood that this project was important to the teachers because it held so much meaning for Zahid. We also understood, by looking at and examining the visuals and the text of the two learning stories, that the high level of storytelling was based upon the care and thought that Isaura and his colleagues had put into collecting the data, photographs, paintings, and dialogue from Zahid's work.

As part of his documentation, Isauro also videotaped Zahid at circle time as Zahid explained in Spanish to the children the definition of "*frontera*" from his personal point of view and his understanding of the U.S. and Mexico border. He highlighted his father's immigration path from Mexico to California, with stops at detention centers in Nebraska and Texas. The combination of the learning story, with its text and visuals, and the video combined to tell a multi-media story of immigration and families across human lives and physical and psychological borders. This multi-modal documentation gave us an important new window on Zahid's family life, his funds of knowledge, his skill in using stories, drawings, maps, books, online information, and his dual language skills to support his learning and to teach his peers and teachers.

Instructional Change and Adaptation

Over time, the inquiry process deepens our understanding of successful literacy strategies for the whole class as well as for individual children. It also helps us realize what a child deserves or might help find helpful at any given moment.

Zahid's "Frontera" Learning Story – Languages, Literacies, Art, and Funds of Knowledge

In the example of Zahid and his deep interest in the word "*frontera*," although it would have been easier to give him the translation, Michael, Alicia, and Sahara realized that it was important to resist looking in the dictionary for the definition – they wanted to draw out the funds of knowledge that they knew that Zahid and the other children already had about families and immigration. They encouraged Zahid to provide his own definition of the word, and in his story to the class at circle time, Zahid talked about his own understanding of the "*frontera*" as a place where people are detained when they come from Mexico to the U.S. Isauro and his co-teachers had not realized that Zahid could do this high level of literacy work, research, explanation, and artistic representation. Although Zahid didn't know how to write the word "*frontera*," he was able to express the concept through the symbolic means of drawing, painting, and storytelling. His interest in one word eventually led Zahid to extend his interest to geography, history, art, and the social context of the meaning of the word.

For Isauro and his co-teachers, their regular use of inquiry, documentation, and reflection provided a systematic process for observing Zahid's learning over time; collecting data on his language, research, and art; and documenting how Zahid shared his learning and extended the funds of knowledge of all of the children. This devotion to inquiry was further deepened through Isauro, Alicia, and Sahara's presentation of Zahid's learning story in our inquiry group meeting. This provided an opportunity for us to hear about how the learning story contained elements of multilingual and multiliteracy learning for Zahid, as well as insights from the teachers regarding how the learning story deepened their instructional supports for Zahid and the other children to learn new and meaningful literacy forms and functions as linked with meaningful events and life challenges.

A Learning Story Entitled "Azel and Tatiana the Turtle" – Inquiry, Narrative, and Curricular Extensions

Zahid's learning story shows how the narrative-based inquiry process can showcase one child's language, literacy, and artistic talents and funds of knowledge. Learning stories can also promote new literacy curriculum possibilities for a small group of children or the whole class. I now present and discuss a complete learning story written by Sahara to Azel, a student in the class who wanted to see the school's turtle. This example shows that what initially starts out as a learning story about one child's experience can turn into a literacy-related project involving several children.

LEARNING STORY – "AZEL AND TATIANA THE TURTLE" BY SAHARA GONZALEZ-GARCIA

What Happened? What Is the History?

Azel, this afternoon when we went out to the patio school yard, you came up to me looking very sad. You tried to tell me something. I asked you what had happened. You did not answer me, you took me by the hand and you led me to where a small group of children gathered in the garden.

A girl, Abigail, explained to me that you wanted to see the turtle but that the children would not let you see it. I asked you if you wanted to see the turtle and you nodded. I told you, "We're going to ask the children to make room for you to see the turtle." We asked for a turn to see it. The children moved and made a space for you to see her up close.

You stayed watching the turtle for a few minutes.

Later, another child offered you some pieces of carrot that were in the garden to feed the turtle. You took the carrot pieces and put them in front of the turtle to eat. You were there for several minutes, patiently and slowly watching how the turtle moved.

After a while, the turtle hid among the plants. "Sleep, mom, dad," you said.

I replied, "Yes, she's going to sleep."

I understood that you were trying to tell me that the turtle was already going to sleep. Glad to have been with the turtle for a while, you went to play in the playground.

– Teacher Sahara

What Does This Action or Activity Mean?

Azel, I've noticed that almost every time we go out into the yard, you go to the garden in search of the turtle. I see that you have a strong interest and great curiosity about the turtle. Sometimes there are many other children who also want to see the turtle and maybe it is difficult for you to ask them to give you a turn or make room for you. Even though you were frustrated you did not hit anyone because they did not give you a turn. You came to me seeking help. That's very good, because you have the ability to self-control and regulate your frustration. Then you welcomed the interaction with other children by feeding the turtle together and sharing the space with you. When the turtle moved away and hid among the plants, you assumed that she was going to sleep. You made use of your critical think-ing. I see how happy you are with the turtle in the garden. We'll continue practicing speech in conversation so you can express yourself when you want to be given a turn if necessary.

What Are Possibilities to Extend the Activity?

We could extend the activity and support Azel's learning by getting books from the library about turtles. We could get fiction and nonfiction books to learn about reptiles. We could also do art activities, sculpt a turtle with playdough, and talk about the body parts of the turtle. Azel, we could also offer you paper and pencils to draw the turtle whenever you observe it. We could also sing songs about the turtle.

To help Azel with his communication efforts, we could use visual cards in different areas of the classroom when he needs help expressing his needs or asking for things. We could also model and invite Azel to repeat complete sentences when he needs help. For example, "Can you give me a turn? Can you help me?"

Response to the Learning Story by Azel's Parents

Hello Saharita,

Thank you very much for sharing this moment of Azel in class with his friends. With all of you he has developed his speech even more and has learned many new things. For example, to play in groups, colors, letters. By spending time with a turtle, he learns more and develops his interest in animals. Maybe the children can take turns in groups to spend time with the turtle and feed her. It could also be that each child takes the turtle home and returns it on Monday. So, at home with their parents, the children can learn together about the turtle. I will get you books on turtles and other materials for the children to use in class and play. What is the turtle's name? What kind of turtle is it? How old is it? Has it reached its maximum size? We could find these answers in a book about turtles. Thank you very much for sharing this beautiful class project.

Ana, Azel's mom

Sahara's learning story, written to Azel, and responded to by Ana, his mother, indicates appropriate next steps for instruction and social interaction to support and extend Azel's interest in the turtle. The learning story, by incorporating elements of setting, character, provocation, dialogue, and photographs, allows Sahara, Azel, and Ana to reflect as a team on the learning possibilities stemming from one small moment when Azel wanted to get close to the turtle, but there were too many children and it was a challenge for him to verbalize what he wanted to do. This small moment or narrative plot point grew into a larger learning process or lesson for Sahara and for Azel's mother, as well as for our entire inquiry group when Sahara presented the learning story with us at one group session. Just as Isauro's learning story about Zahid revealed Zahid's use of literacy to extend his understanding of the word "*frontera*," Sahara's story to Azel also opened up new possibilities for language and literacy teaching and learning.

Further, when Sahara shared her learning story written to Azel in our inquiry group, we realized that Ana, Azel's mother had made several excellent suggestions in her learning story response, which ranged from having children take turns taking the turtle home on weekends to bringing turtle books into the classroom. Sahara explained to us that when she and Isauro and Alicia met with the children, they discussed Ana's ideas as well as their own ideas for curricular extensions, which ranged from getting books from the library or bookmobile about turtles to sculpting turtles with playdough to making a painting of turtles with watercolors or acrylic. Based on their conversation with the children, the teachers decided to bring in a number of fiction and nonfiction books about turtles for informal book browsing, whole-group and small-group read-alouds, discussion and research, and for use with observational drawings of the turtle.

The children's first observational drawings of the turtle were based on direct observations during a small-group activity in the garden outside the classroom. The children also had the opportunity to make drawings of the turtle when the teachers brought her to visit the classroom. They put the turtle on a table so that the children could observe it closely and see the details of its shell and its movements.

BRIAN: The turtle walks very slowly.
LUNA: The turtle has four legs.
LUCAS: Tatiana's shell has shapes that look like squares of various colors.

Several children wanted to carry out a series of observational drawings of the turtle. Isauro observed that Abigail (Figure 6.3) and other children observed the turtle with extreme care and tried to draw the shape of the turtle's body and facial expression.

As their observations became more intentional, the children's drawings became more detailed. Children such Brian (Figures 6.4 and 6.5) and Gael (Figures 6.6, 6.7, and 6.8) drew with great concentration and intentionality as they tried to capture the shells and the limbs with accuracy and realism.

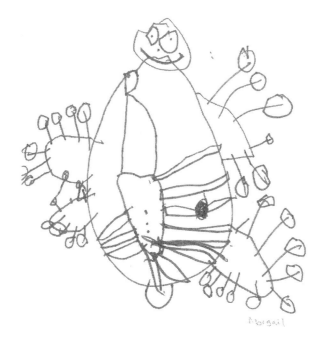

FIGURE 6.3   Abigail's Turtle Drawing

FIGURE 6.4   Brian's First Turtle Drawing

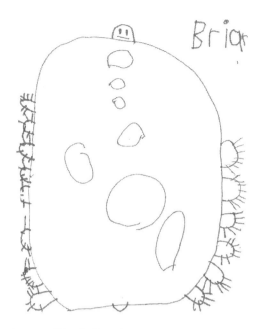

FIGURE 6.5 Brian's Second Turtle Drawing

FIGURE 6.6 Gael Composing His First Turtle Drawing

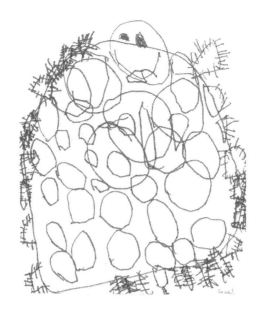

FIGURE 6.7 Gael's First Turtle Drawing

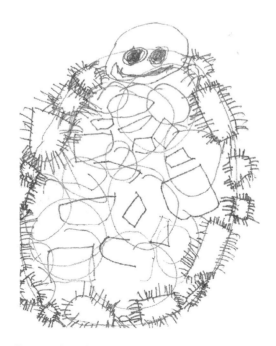

FIGURE 6.8 Gael's Second Turtle Drawing

Isauro noticed that Gael, who did not like to trace letters on ditto sheets, created representation drawings of the turtle that revealed the depth of his observations and the tremendous effort he made to capture the intricate design of the turtle's shell on two separate occasions.

Other children also developed a more refined style in their drawing, and added more detail through more careful observation and discussion with peers and the teachers. Lucas created a series that increased in detail (Figures 6.9 and 6.10) as did Luna (Figures 6.11 and 6.12).

FIGURE 6.9 Lucas's First Turtle Drawing

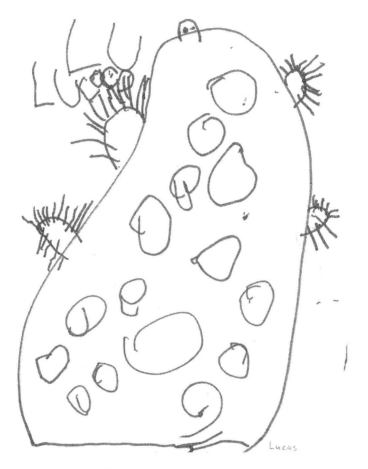

FIGURE 6.10   Lucas's Second Turtle Drawing

While these children carried out their observational drawings, other children wanted to "read" the nonfiction and fiction books about turtles that the teachers had brought into the classroom, and other children such as Azel wanted to paint small turtles on cardboard that his mother had sent in to the classroom. The cardboard turtles were displayed in the classroom on a shelf along with the fiction and nonfiction turtle books.

When Isauro presented the series of observational drawings to our inquiry group, he highlighted the developmental and symbolic progression from the children's initial observation to their more sophisticated artistic representation. The sharing of these drawings, and the telling of the story behind their creation via the learning story, revealed to us the underlying developmental progression of the children's evolving abilities and talents for moving from observation to representation. We also saw the specific talents and abilities of individual children from a

FIGURE 6.11 Luna's First Turtle Drawing

new, strength-based perspective, as this was the first time that we had observed and discussed such detailed and thoughtful observational drawings. The learning story also enabled us to see how the children combined their interest in science and nature with their literacy talents for book sharing, discussion, brainstorming, drawing, and painting. Last, we witnessed how the learning story involved Ana, Azel's mother, and how the response to Azel about his learning story revealed Ana's own curricular ideas, in essence her funds of knowledge for supporting her son's literacy interests and skills.

Luna

FIGURE 6.12 Luna's Second Turtle Drawing

Chapter Summary and Closing

In this chapter, I described and explained a number of key elements for breaking down our understanding of inquiry, documentation, and reflection. I also provided a larger professional context for this process by showing how the inquiry process can be powerfully integrated into regularly scheduled inquiry group meetings. I strongly believe from my many years of this work that inquiry groups are instrumental for creating, nurturing, and tinkering with the inquiry process for teachers (and coaches, other ECE educators, and families), and for promoting a positive climate of professional trust, dialogue, and collaboration.

Inquiry groups provide a public, communal forum that challenge us to bring our "best" documentation and inquiry ideas to the group meetings, and to receive positive, constructive feedback not only on our inquiry work but also on next steps for teaching, instruction, social relationships, and partnerships with families. The key element is the marrying of high-quality documentation with intentional, thoughtful professional dialogue, which results in an evolving sense of the group as a powerful source for the healthy exchange of inquiry and teaching ideas, and a public space for highlighting the interests, talents, and abilities of young children of Color.

As the learning stories discussed toward of the end of this chapter indicate, the passion and funds of knowledge of children of Color (as seen in Isauro's learning story about Zahid and his passion for the word "*frontera*," and Sahara's learning story about Azel and the turtle, which turned into a long-term project) challenge us as educators to see the language and literacy talents of children of Color in a more authentic and powerful light. And it's the inquiry process that propels this illumination, raising our awareness and knowledge of the literacy talents of children of Color, the literacy and funds of knowledge of families, and own literacy knowledge as educators.

Over time, the involvement in an inquiry group melds the personal and professional. For example, it was uplifting and empowering – personally, professionally, politically – to observe, document, share, and critique Sahara's learning story about Zahid's interest in the word "*frontera*." Our inquiry group felt that we gained a valuable lesson on history, immigration, culture, family, and language from Zahid's interest, his dual language exploration and research in books, and his symbolic expression via painting, drawing, and mapmaking. This learning story resonated with all of our group members, and it was especially meaningful for the majority of the members of our group who are multilingual speakers with immigrant, transnational roots. Zahid's interest in the word "*frontera*" and Azel's interest in the turtle were their gifts to us, small moments in their daily participation in classrooms that we enlarged and magnified through inquiry, documentation, narrative, and reflection.

CLOSING REFLECTIONS

- What have you learned from this chapter that has deepened your understanding of the important forms and functions of teacher inquiry?
- Which aspects of documentation in the chapter do you find most appealing, and why?
- What do you now think of integrating inquiry, documentation, and reflection within the communal, professional forum of regularly scheduled inquiry group meetings?

- What do you see as the value of narrative for deepening our inquiry, documentation, and reflection?
- What are a few short-term next steps that you'd now like to take to deepen and broaden your inquiry work on your own and with colleagues?

References

Goeson, R. (2014). Finding our voices through narrative inquiry: Exploring a conflict of cultures. *Voices of Practitioners, 9*(1), 1–22.

Meier, D. with Chavez, E., Mancina, J., & Eung, L. (2017). Zaida T. Rodriguez early education school – "Telling a story on the walls." In L. K. Kroll & D. R. Meier (Eds.), *Documentation and inquiry in the early childhood classroom: Research stories of engaged practitioners in urban centers and school* (pp. 74–90). New York, NY: Routledge.

Sisk-Hilton, S., & Meier, D. R. (2016). *Narrative inquiry in early childhood and elementary school: Learning to teach, teaching well.* New York: Routledge.

Stremmel, A. (2014). The power of narrative inquiry to transform both teacher and mentor. *Voices of Practitioners, 9*(1), 1–5.

7

TAKING ACTION – NEXT STEPS TOWARD A STRENGTH-BASED LITERACY EDUCATION

In this final chapter, I recap where we've travelled together in this book, and then highlight important next steps for further strengthening the literacy education of young children of Color and their families. As you read this final chapter, please consider your own journey through this book, and note those ideas, theories, and practices that you have found most valuable and want to pursue further. I wish you well in your continuing journey.

Key Themes – Awareness, Excellence, and Visibility

In this book's Introduction, I described and discussed certain longstanding images of children of Color that contribute to a deficit view of their literacy talents as well as those of their families. I also highlighted how the central themes of this book – deepening our awareness, achieving high levels of excellence, and increased visibility – are at the foundation of strength-based literacy education. Deepening our *awareness* refers to our efforts, individual and collective, to recognize our own language and literacy talents, as well as those of children and families of Color. Awareness is not a first step nor a precondition in moving toward actualizing a strength-based preschool literacy education; rather, it demands that we continually deepen and sharpen our awareness of the literacy talents of children and families of Color over our entire educational careers. Achieving high levels of *excellence* refers to our high-literacy curriculum and instruction, which includes such key factors as how we conceptualize a powerful literacy education and the design of the learning environment to our specific literacy tools and strategies. Excellence also refers to our daily and lifelong goals for children of Color – that we expect, support, and delight in their academic excellence as children whose social, cultural, and linguistic talents are the foundation for reaching new heights in their literacy development.

Increased *visibility* involves elevating the image of young children of Color and their families in positive ways in classrooms, schools, and beyond. Part of this process necessitates elevating our own image as highly knowledgeable, agentic, and committed educators who want to share our literacy expertise with and learn from our colleagues through the professional process of reflection, documentation, and inquiry.

Making the Research Our Own

A first action step in strengthening our literacy teaching involves making the relevant theory and research our own. In Chapter 1, I told the story of selected theory and research on the language and literacy development of young children over the last 40 years, and I highlighted how this research has strengthened my conceptual foundation for understanding and supporting the literacy talents of young children of Color. I also noted how I have lived through and experienced much of this history starting from my early teaching and graduate school work in the early 1980s and continuing through my current work as a teacher educator, part-time preschool literacy teacher, and facilitator and participant in teacher inquiry groups.

There are a number of important threads from this research story that I emphasized throughout this book. For instance, I discussed the critical role of children's funds of knowledge, which includes the linguistic and literacy knowledge learned from home, community, and school. It is important for us, then, to remain mindful of the sensitive, nuanced, and human nature of literacy learning for young children, and to see where and how we can integrate children's evolving knowledge into our literacy philosophies, practices, and interactions.

It is also helpful to tinker with our philosophy of literacy education, and continually search for new ideas and practices for formulating and taking action on behalf of a strength-based literacy education for young children of Color. For example, for many years I was deeply influenced by progressive educational thinkers who emphasize child-directed play and open-ended discovery in preschool literacy education, and this perspective remains an important foundation for my literacy teaching. But I have also learned to integrate specific aspects of directed literacy teaching such as alphabetic knowledge, sound-symbol correspondence, and concepts of print within child- and culturally responsive literacy activities and processes.

For example, as described in Chapter 5, I look for specific moments with certain children where I can pinpoint aspects of literacy skill and knowledge in whole-class read-alouds and the small-group activities of drawing and dictation in their personal journals. In this effort, I am mindful of returning to the value of my work in the early 1980s in Jean Chall's reading lab, and how passionately Chall exhorted us to emphasize vocabulary meanings as well as vocabulary within the context of the text. At the same, I also return to Lisa Delpit's call in the late 1980s for increased and equitable access to the codes of power for children of Color in their literacy learning, and the value of clear, direct instruction regarding the most highly prized school-based forms and functions of literacy.

I have learned, too, to integrate aspects of research begun in earnest in the 1990s by Gloria Ladson-Billings and others focusing on culturally responsive education and the power of high-quality, multicultural children's literature. I am now a more intentional researcher and collector of children's books that fit this framework, and more adept at finding effective ways to use these books with children in varied contexts and for varied literacy purposes. I have also turned to more recent research on critical race theory, asset pedagogies, and generative spaces from H. Samy Alim and others to deepen my awareness of how race, racism, identity, and power also influence how we conceptualize and implement a strength-based approach for children of Color.

I encourage, you, then, to return to Chapter 1 and other chapters in this book to note and reflect on the ideas and strategies of certain thinkers and approaches that you'd like to pursue more deeply in your literacy teaching.

The Perspectives of Families

Families are often the forgotten partners in a successful strength-based approach for young children of Color. As I discussed in Chapter 2, I spoke with several families of Color, who spoke passionately and with deep knowledge about their children's literacy talents and abilities. The families talked about the elements of preschool literacy instruction that supported their children, and they also made suggestions for improving preschool literacy curriculum and classroom instruction for their children and other children of Color. The families described how they supported their children's language and literacy learning at home and in the community, and explained the values, beliefs, and reasons behind their literacy goals and practices.

Literacy Success Over Time

Some families with older children took a long developmental view of their children's literacy learning beyond preschool, and described how they have extended and built upon their children's preschool literacy education.

The families had long-term goals for their children's literacy learning and for their academic success in general. This is a helpful reminder, that a strength-based literacy education for young children of Color goes beyond the preschool years; it's lifelong literacy learning and success. For instance, Jamal and Charemon, parents of five-year-old Cameron and ten-year-old Jamilla, strongly share college as a goal for both of their children and an advanced degree as well.

JAMAL: We are both quite clear that literacy, learning to read and write, along with math, are *gatekeepers* to academic success and social success. We expect them to do well in school, get a job and a career, and to be self-sufficient.

They believe that attaining these long-terms goals for their children are largely based on their children's literacy achievement, and they actively support their children's literacy at home and have chosen an Afro-centric independent school for its cultural and educational responsiveness.

Expanding Languages and Literacies

The families are also devoted to promoting multilingualism and multiliteracies in their homes. For example, Lidia, the parent of four-year-old Julian and seven-year-old Isaiaa, supports Spanish and English at home with her two children. She also noted that Isaiaa takes an active interest in bringing preschool books in Spanish home for reading, and she and her husband are working to increase their use of Spanish at home in conversation and in book sharing and reading. Although Julian and Isaiaa do not understand everything that their parents say in Spanish, Lidia and her husband are committed to persevering in their increased use of Spanish at home.

Challenges for Families

The families also spoke of a range of challenges to literacy and school success for their children of Color. For example, Haneefah, a parent of two African-American boys, nine-year-old Ismail and three-year-old Jacob, discussed the misperceptions and stereotypes that her children face in school as African-American children. Haneefah is concerned that her children are "forced into a box" of conforming to expectations about how they should act and think in school because they are African-American boys. Haneefah believes that her children are expected to adhere to the dominant European way of acting and thinking in public school classrooms, which doesn't always apply to Ismail and Jacob's ways of thinking, talking, and interacting, as well as their literacy interests, talents, and abilities. As Haneefah put it, "Their schools send my children the message that you must play it safe and just show us that you can do enough." But as a concerned and supportive parent, who is keenly aware that her children can be labeled as "misbehaving," Haneefah wants a more authentic and deeper vision of her children's abilities and identities.

The Perspectives of Educators

In Chapter 3, I presented the experiences, perspectives, and lived experiences of a number of passionate and talented educators of Color. These are all educators whom I know well, and admire their dedication, knowledge, and political will to understand and support preschool children of Color. As I discussed earlier in this book, I spoke with these educators and featured their experiences and perspectives early in this book because they complement and extend my teaching ideas and practices as a Jewish/White male that I have presented throughout this book, and most prominently in Chapters 4, 5, and 6.

Languages, Literacies, and Power

The educators shared their hopes, dreams, and practices working and supporting children and families of Color. Some educators, like Carlos Castillejo, take a decidedly philosophical and political view of a strength-based perspective on the literacy learning of preschool children of Color. Carlos argues for greater control of the forms and functions of languages and literacies for educators, children, and their families, and is passionate about linking this control with increased power for all of us to influence the content and delivery of preschool literacy learning.

Carlos asks, "If the school always controls the language that is taught, then who owns the language? Who owns the power?" Carlos, like a number of the other educators with whom I spoke, recognizes that high-quality literacy education for young children of Color includes basic literacy knowledge, but it goes far beyond this somewhat low-level curricular and educational goal. In this respect, Carlos and the educators remind us that literacy education is only as effective as our entire approach to preschool education, which must include our literacy philosophy of education as well as a toolbox of literacy practices for "changing the relations of power" to "acknowledge and support" the social, cultural, and literacy talents of children of Color.

Valuing Our Own Histories and Identities

For Dawn Douangsawang, conceptualizing and enacting a strength-based view of literacy education demands that we confront our most persistent biases and misperceptions, as well as holding on to our most treasured values around languages and literacies to contribute to personal, individual, social, and communal change and transformation.

Dawn was born and raised in the San Francisco Bay area, and was not allowed to use English at home growing up as her parents highly prized maintaining their Laotian culture and language. She remembers listening to many oral stories in Lao growing up, and now values her parents' insistence on not losing their Laotian culture. But when she entered kindergarten at a public school, Dawn had a friend with whom she spoke Lao in the classroom. Their kindergarten teacher discouraged their speaking Lao, and Dawn became quiet and withdrawn, fearing that the teachers and children would laugh at her for not knowing a certain English word.

Dawn, like the other educators I spoke with, remembers these and other pivotal school memories around languages, literacies, and identities. These memories stay with us our entire lives, and Dawn uses these painful memories as a reminder to understand her preschool students and their families, and to conceptualize and enact a literacy education where her children's languages and literacies have personal, individual, and cultural import and value. As Dawn put it, "Deep down, I know their language has meaning."

Inquiry and Reflection

The educators also value the process of inquiry, documentation, and reflection for providing ongoing professional development and growth both for themselves and for their colleagues. They see the process and practice of reflection as fundamental for continuously learning to recognize the literacy strengths and talents of young children of Color and their families, as well as their own talents for literacy teaching and relationship-building.

Isauro Michael Escamilla deeply believes in the power of inquiry, documentation, and reflection for deepening his philosophy of literacy education and improving his literacy teaching. Working with Isauro and his colleagues in our monthly inquiry group over the last several years, I have witnessed how the inquiry process elevates our observational skills, data collection and analysis abilities, and talent for representing children's literacy insights and achievements through varied forms of documentation. I've also witnessed how this process provides concrete evidence to educators of our talents for recognizing and making visible in a communal, public manner the achievements of young children of Color and their families. As the early childhood field continues to face challenges in terms of a lack of resources and professional development opportunities, teacher inquiry and reflection is a promising, home-grown way of teaching and of living in schools that deepens and strengthens our literacy teaching.

Integrating and Adapting Literacy Practices

The literacy practices that I have described in varied ways in this book are designed to show possibilities for you as the reader to pick and choose which best suit you and your teaching context. As I discussed earlier in this book, we are at a point in literacy research, theory, and practice where we must take more ownership for conceptualizing and implementing literacy programs and approaches that we can adapt to who we are as individuals, as community members, and as educators in specific local contexts.

If you are reading and using this book as a preservice early childhood educator in an A.A., B.A., or M.A. program, or reading this book on your own, review your notes from this book's chapters and the opening and closing reflective prompts. Identify those key ideas and practices that you find most appealing and doable, and try out a few in your teaching placements or hold onto some for your future teaching. Link this book on the literacy talents of young children of Color with your other studies on diversity, equity, critical thinking, anti-bias education, and culturally responsive education. Over time, and with trial-and-error, your instructional toolkit for understanding and supporting young children of Color will expand and deepen.

If you teach in a Head Start program using Creative Curriculum or another approach, a Bright Horizons program using World at Their Fingertips™, or a site with your own "home-grown" literacy curriculum, look for those small places and moments of teaching and learning with children and families of Color where you can integrate elements and ideas from this book. If you are a new teacher, take a few of the most promising literacy ideas and practices from this book, and see how and where you can adapt and integrate them over the course of a year. For example, maybe your goal is to strengthen your use of high-quality, culturally responsive read-alouds and you will choose a few ideas and practices from Chapter 4. If you are a veteran teacher, maybe you are interested in linking whole-class read-alouds with small-group book browsing, conversation, and drawing and dictation in children's personal journals. For this goal, look again at Chapters 4 and 5 and pinpoint those specific ideas and strategies that you find most interesting and relevant. For both novice and more veteran teachers, whatever new literacy goals and practices you choose as next steps, I strongly suggest adding in a healthy dose of inquiry, documentation, and reflection to document and assess the next chapter in your literacy journey. I urge you to work with your administration, coaches, funders, and other partners to implement regular inquiry group meetings for sharing and obtaining feedback on your literacy inquiry and documentation.

Closing

It is often said that all great teaching is deeply personal. And I hope you have felt that what I have written in this book – from my discussion of relevant literacy theory and research to my discussions with colleagues and families to the presentation of my literacy work with young children in the classroom – is deeply personal. In this respect, we work with preschool children of Color out of a strong desire to recognize and support their literacy talents and abilities, as well as those of their families. And we must do so in smart, thoughtful ways, creating and implementing and constantly refining our approaches, practices, and strategies. Hope and desire and awareness are critical, though not enough. We need to match and meld our deep desire to strengthen the literacy learning of children of Color with high-quality, rigorous, and illuminating teaching. I am reminded, as I close here, of a remark from a preschooler with whom I once worked. Tashawn asked me for one of his favorite children's books, and I reached into my bookbag on the floor, searched for it, and then realized it was not there. I told him that I didn't have it. "Mr. Meier," he said, "You gotta keep up with your stuff." It's a never-ending journey, and I hope that you have found this book of value personally and professionally. I wish you well in your continuing teaching and supporting the literacy talents and abilities of young children of Color and their families.

Appendix

BACKGROUND OF EDUCATORS AND FAMILIES PROFILED IN THE BOOK

Name	Background
Prenties Brown	Head Start preschool teacher with coaching responsibilities. Pursuing an M.A. in early childhood education.
Maria Carriedo	ECE Principal, Spanish/English educator. Married to Tony, Sr. Parent of Tony, Jr. (age 6) and twins (age 3), who attend public schools.
Carlos Castillejo	Spanish/English dual language preschool teacher. M.A. in early childhood education.
Jamal Cooks	Married to Charemon; children: Jamilla (age 10), Cameron (age 5), who attend an Afro-centric independent P–8 school.
Shyla Crowder	Parent of Exavier (age 7) and a second child (age 4).
Dawn Douangsawang	Preschool teacher, Lao/English. M.A. in early childhood education.
Isauro Michael Escamilla	Dual language Spanish/English preschool teacher. M.A. in early childhood education and currently pursuing an Ed.D. in educational leadership.
Amanda Ibarra	Preschool teacher, Spanish and English.
Gaya Kekulawela	Preschool teacher, Sinhala and English. M.A. in early childhood education.
Ambreen Khawaja	Head Start supervisor.
Dale Long	25 years of experience as a public school preschool teacher.
Alma Lyons	Head Start preschool teacher, English/Tagalog.
Mr. Jon Sims	Head Start preschool teacher, English.

(*Continued*)

(Continued)

Name	Background
Hannah Nguyen	Head Start preschool teacher and Montessori preschool teacher, English/Vietnamese.
Haneefah Shuaibe-Peters	Executive director of an independent preschool. M.A. in early childhood education and currently an Ed.D. in educational leadership. Parent of Jacob (age 5) and Ismail (age 8).
Lidia Silas	Parent of Julian (age 5) and Isaiaa (age 8). Occupation: nurse.
Maria Sujo	Kindergarten readiness manager for Oakland Unified School District, and teacher educator. Spanish/English. M.A. in early childhood education.

INDEX

Note: Page numbers in *italics* indicate a figure.

and literacy 33; non-traditional literacy practices at home 37–38; practices 35–36
Freire, Paulo 10–11
"frontera" learning 133–143
funds of knowledge 11, 98–99, 133

Garcia, Ofelia 14–15
generative pedagogy 10
generative spaces 19–20
Graves, Donald 7
Gregory, Eve 15–17

Heath, Shirley Brice 9
high-quality literacy education 54; adapting curriculum to fit children's needs 57–60; culturally responsive teaching 55–57; developmentally responsive teaching 54–55
histories 150

identities 150; histories and 150; as scholar 31–32
influential research and theory 9
inquiry 20–22, 151
instructional change 132–143
instructional elements 80; children's curiosity and imagination 81–83; interest in others and world 83–84; whole-class read-alouds 80–81

journals 60; *see also* personal journals; reflective teaching journals

kindergarten 4, 36–38, 48–49, 53–54, 96, 150
knowledge: funds of 11–12, 15; of literacy conventions 107–109; literacy talents and funds of 53

language 20–21, 136, 150; knowledge 6; and literacy 4, 35; philosophy of 47
Language Experience Approach 6–7
Laotian culture 48–49
learning 51–52; formats and groupings 6; foundational philosophies of 46, 48–49; power of 48; to read 5; step-by-step model of 6; stories 21, 62
liberatory education 10
linking inquiry 61–63
literacy 150; challenges 35; children's knowledge of 56; community 84; curriculum 48, 59; development 4,

31; emergent 5–6; engagement and learning 122–123; experience of 51; in formal school settings 8; goal of 81; inside-out and outside-in approaches to 17; instruction 6; learning and development 8; mixed-aged interactions around 15–16; multilingualism and 33; pedagogies 8; practices 41, 151–152; strengths 59; teaching and learning 31
literacy curricula, effective 59
literacy education 3; childhood 3–4; permeable boundaries in 14; philosophy of 47; of preschool children of Color 46; retrospective views on 31; strength-based approach to 8; *see also* educator perspectives on literacy education
literacy learning 10–11, 31, 36, 53; children's sociocultural resources for 13; foundation for 36–37; terms of 53
literacy teaching 4, 123, 136; approach to 59; direct and indirect 38–40; passion and talents for 60; Spanish on 52
literary patterns in text and visuals 106–107
Long, Dale 59

McNamee, Gillian 14
Milner, H. Richard 19–20
Moll, Luis 11
multicultural/multilingual books 71
multilingualism 14, 32, 33
multilingual learning 17, 133
multiliteracy learning 14, 133

narratives 130–131
new language learners 15–17
New Zealand 21, 57
Nimmo, John 11–12
non-traditional literacy 37–38

objects 110, *113*
observational drawing 101
oral language 103–105

Paley, Vivian 14
Paris, Django 19–20
pedagogy of listening 20
peer-to-peer book sharing 84; child-initiated engagement 87–89; opportunities to practice and extend 85–87; read-aloud books 84–85
personal journals 95–97, 109; drawing in 101; elements of 97
Pinkney, Jerry 72–75, 100–101

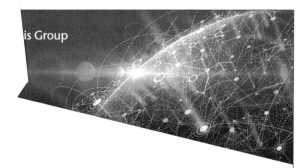